DOVER
FRONT

A
SEARCHLIGHT
REPORTER
BOOK

DOVER FRONT

BY

REGINALD FOSTER

Special Correspondent of the " Daily Herald "
at Dover since May 1940

LONDON

SECKER & WARBURG

1941

Martin Secker & Warburg Ltd.
22 Essex Street, London, W.C.2

First Published July 1941

MADE AND PRINTED IN GREAT BRITAIN BY
MORRISON AND GIBB LTD., LONDON AND EDINBURGH

CONTENTS

LIST OF ILLUSTRATIONS

MY THANKS are due to the Editor and News
Editor of the *Daily Herald*, who made it possible
for me to see the beginning and end of some
of our country's greatest days, and who have
allowed me to use here some of the material
gathered on their behalf.   R. F.

FOREWORD

ALL through those long and magnificent days of the August of 1940 we sat on the Dover Cliffs and watched the great battles in the air. We had come to the coast of Kent from the newspaper offices of New York and Chicago and Washington, and from Melbourne, Toronto and London, from all the English-speaking countries. Those battles over the corner of England changed us—particularly they changed us who had come to Dover from the United States. The world began to shrink about us from America as we saw men fighting so fast in such great areas of space. All the measurements that we had ever known dwindled. What were channels any more? And what were oceans?

As we saw British airmen flying into German formations, ten and even twenty times their size, we forgot that we were Americans who had come to England to watch—we were in England from then on to pray. We were in the presence of the most exalted bravery and personal courage, and suddenly we found ourselves closer to the United States in England than we had ever been at home. Suddenly we saw that we were where we were, and we had what we had, because a long line of our people had been willing to die. We realised at Dover what Valley Forge and Gettysburg were. We understood a new meaning of home.

My friend, Reg Foster, has well recorded those days, and as an American I am very proud to be asked to write a Foreword for this record of an English colleague.

BEN ROBERTSON.

The Newspaper P.M.
NEW YORK.

CHAPTER ONE

DOVER ROAD TO THE WAR

THE fortune of war, a telephone call, and a day journey
into Kent combined to start me on the road that was to
lead to Dover on a sunny morning, 22 May 1940. I never
returned home that night as intended, and now, a year
later, I am still on the Dover Front. It has been a strange
year, in which I have seen the making and passing of
history. Luck, and a certain newspaper man's intuition,
took me to the place which was for a short time to become
the most exciting war centre in the world. Now, in
May 1941, Dover waits any further developments with
something of the stolidity of the veteran soldier.

The Nazi invasion of the West had begun on 10 May.
But in those early Spring days the word *Blitz* had not
become current coin in the English vocabulary. True,
Holland had already collapsed, but no one knew that in
less than a month the nation was to be first shocked and
then heartened by the events of Dunkirk. No one knew
that the slow drift of the war was to become a breathless
gallop and that the 'Battle of Britain' was even then
coming up over the horizon, across the Straits of Dover.
Mass raids and 'Fire Blitz' days were far away. People
still talked about the 'Bore War', but the fall of Holland
and the swift collapse of Belgium had even then opened
the way to untold events.

I had already made another journey into Kent on that
same day, 10 May, to search for the first bombs of the war
dropped on England. It was later reported that Nazi

9

aircraft had dropped twenty-four incendiary and twenty high explosive bombs in the neighbourhood of the little village of Chilham, near Canterbury. We walked through woods looking for the small finned incendiary bombs and were excited when we found one. From the direction of the Thames Estuary there came the sound of distant gunfire, and that in itself was sufficiently unusual in those days to make us pause and listen. War, as it was later to become, had not yet visited this country.

That then was the background when my telephone rang on 22 May. It was a day off and I was at home, pottering about in the garden and wondering if there would be any cricket the following Saturday. It was like that, in those days.

Some reporters never answer the telephone on their day off. I have always done so, taking the gamble that the ring might lead to a big story. Sometimes of course you are disappointed, but by then it is too late. ' They ' would like you to go to the London office because someone is ill or ' they ' want you to do something that seems both dull and uninteresting. But peace-time adventures, like the Cheltenham torso mystery, the great Fen floods, the ' Ellen Ruddle Riddle ' at Bath, the Mona Tinsley kidnapping case and many others, had come to me out of a telephone call—and you never could tell what your luck might be.

This particular call did not at first sight seem to promise anything very unusual. Neither the *Daily Herald* office nor myself had any reason to believe it would lead me to the evacuation of the British Expeditionary Force, to the biggest air battles in history, with hundreds of aircraft engaged, to the shelling of Dover, fantastic months in the Grand Hotel and the whole series of historic days that became known as the ' Battle of Britain '. It may well be indeed that history will record these sunny summer months, when there was storm in the air day and night, as the most critical of the war.

The voice on the telephone suggested it might be a good idea if I were to take the car out into Kent and write about the first newly formed ' Paratroops ', the men who responded so eagerly to that suggestion for home defence put out by the British Legion. The voice seemed to insinuate that it was a nice day, that I was doing nothing important and in any case could get back early in the evening, and that the free day would be made up later.

There seemed no reason why that should not be the programme. I kissed my wife, who was always disappointed when I went off on these sudden missions, said good-bye to Christopher, whom I have seen only twice since, said blithely I would be home about seven in the evening, with a mental reservation for ten, and set off to nowhere in particular.

I reached the Canterbury road and decided that Canterbury would be as good a place as any to find out what was happening about this reported birth of a volunteer defence movement which was later to become one of our strongest defences. I had previously spent two or three weeks in that town, covering a murder. I had a number of contacts there who would know about the first recruiting of Paratroops.

The car and I reached Canterbury about noon. In the "*Fleur de Lis*" I saw the big shambling form of H. L. McNally, of the *Daily Express*. That casual meeting was the beginning of my trip to Dover and all that it came to mean. Mac told me he had been in this area of Kent, for various reasons, since the Chilham bombs.

" And now," he said, in his Irish brogue, " they have just told me to go to Dover and stay there. They don't seem to know why."

I did not know either and I even doubt whether the

Daily Express did. But the diversion to Dover seemed as good an idea as any and I thought the Paratroop situation might be even more interesting there. Dover also had the advantage of being a little further away from the office and possibly a little nearer the war. I believe that, right from the beginning, there had been a secret determination at the back of my mind to go to Dover. Its very position seemed to indicate that as the war moved nearer the coast of France and Belgium, the town would become a key point.

Dover was still peaceful at this time, with its record of eight Alerts, or ' syreens ' as everyone called them there. Enemy aircraft were rarely seen. Now, twelve months later, the Alert figure has passed the thousand mark.

On this day of 22 May we were unknowingly only a week from the miracle of Dunkirk—rather less, because the evacuation was first ordered on 26 May. But the enemy forces were thrusting through France with incredible speed, and making their encircling sweep to the coast more rapidly than anyone realised.

I think the innocent arrival of McNally and myself at Dover was regarded with some suspicion by the local military authorities, who knew a good deal more than we did of the real situation developing after the break-through by the Germans in the Sedan sector. But neither of us had any inkling of the sights we would see in a week, and Dunkirk was only a name on the map of France.

McNally could only say with truth he did not know why he had been sent to Dover, because the town did not then appear to be in the news. My own presence was even more the result of chance, yet something in the atmosphere made me decide to stay. And in fact, as the news came through from France, almost each hour that passed brought signs of increasing tension.

This tension was reflected in the early attitude of the

authorities. Once, after a day or two, I received a mid-night telephone call from high authority at Dover Castle. It seemed I had been reported for talking to naval officers. This was rather odd, because I was being particularly circumspect in my dealings with the services. True, I had been in brisk conversation with an officer, to whom I had been casually introduced by a civilian as the *Daily Herald* special correspondent. To my surprise the naval officer reacted considerably. " Hallo," he said, " glad to meet you. I'm Co-op." The reference did not mean anything to me and I lamely replied " Oh yes."

" Yes," he said, " you ought to know, damned if you didn't." " Oh well," I went on, " I never take any interest in Service people's jobs. I have to be very careful, you know."

The naval officer was still more annoyed. He explained that he had been an executive in the Co-operative move-ment before the war and he naturally considered that as a *Daily Herald* man I would be interested. But I was careful, and later it took me days to placate him and convince him that my seeming ignorance was not studied. Yet another officer who overheard part of the conversation must have regarded it with suspicion. It became equally difficult for me to convince Authority of my innocence.

We newspaper reporters were not popular with the authorities in those pre-Dunkirk days, and now I know why. They knew the plight of the B.E.F., and imagined we had more information on the matter than we had, and possibly more than we had any right to. It accounted for the hostility displayed by a naval commander who has since become one of our good friends. He and McNally and myself had a vigorous argument concerning the rights of the Press in general which developed into a slanging match, with no quarter on either side. The authorities had taken no chances at that time, and were taking none.

As I went to telephone from the back parlour of a country inn, five miles from Dover, an Army Security officer walked in and asked to see my papers. He wanted to know what I was telephoning and to whom. He also preferred to stay and listen. Dover was not then as Press conscious as now, when it has been visited by scores of War Correspondents, special correspondents, special writers, reporters, cinema men, photographers and radio men from all over the world.

On the next morning, 23 May, having given the office some adequate explanation why I had stayed overnight, I went on with the 'Parashot' story. Parashot stories were still few, the great Home Guard organisation months away. But I did a very neat story, it seemed, with a nice historical allusion to the Black Prince, who was christened in what would now be called a 'front line' church, and a reference to the spirit of Queen Eleanor being reborn in that centuries-old farmhouse which men of to-day were preparing to defend again. But the office apparently considered that there was too much real history brewing to be interested in the Black Prince. The story was not used, and the next day I thought about returning to London and the comfortable boredom of those early war days.

There seemed to me no savour at this time in ordinary 'peace-time news'. Dunkirk was not even a whisper, not to us at any rate, and all day on the 24th there was talk of a counter-attack, which, delivered at the right time, would turn the enemy. But there was no effective counter-attack, and the Germans swept on.

There were the beginnings of air activity—these were the days when a night warning was news. At this time everything stopped for an Alert. Telephoning became impossible and the authorities encouraged a stop-every-thing-and-go-to-ground policy. The game for us corre-spondents was to leap on the telephone at the first wail of

the siren and try and persuade the operator to pass a
call. Remember, air-raids had not begun then, Dover
had not been bombed or shelled, and the sight of a Jerry
aircraft was something approaching a sensation.

So, with one development and the other, I stayed on
at Dover " another day ".

Saturday the 25th brought the first considerable air
activity of the war at Dover, when *Heinkel* seaplanes
tried to lay mines outside the harbour. There was a good
anti-aircraft barrage, flaming onions and a violent explosion
in the air indicated the destruction of an enemy machine
at sea. We thought we were seeing the war !

Across the Channel the battle for Dunkirk was in progress, but even yet we did not realise its full significance.
Windows and doors rattled from continuous gunfire. By
day and night there were explosions and rumblings. All
the time women and children were playing on the shingle
of Dover. At night, from up on the cliffs, people could
see rifle- and gunfire from the beaches across the Straits of
Dover. The first account of this given to the world was a
broadcast given for the Canadian Broadcasting Corpora-
tion by Tom Moore, landlord of a cliff-top inn that later
became our headquarters. In that script he described
how he could see the war and at night pick out the flicker-
ing gun flashes that showed where our men and the enemy
were in action along the coast.

It was still almost a normal peace-time summer, but
twenty miles away, across the Straits, our men were in a
more desperate plight than we knew. The Channel ports
we then held were being heavily attacked from the air.
The " Maid of Kent ", once favourite Channel packet,
and now converted into a hospital ship, was set on fire
on 21 May, but it was some days before the news leaked
through Dover. In fact three hospital ships were lost
through bombing in this period, including the " Brighton "

and " Paris ", and with them were lost a number of Dover men. But still Dunkirk had not started and Dover's greatest and most frightening days were still to come.

The news was bad in Flanders, but when the London office said to me on the telephone, " You may see the return of the B.E.F." it was a grim, rather bitter gesture rather than a serious belief. It was still thought the B.E.F. could extricate itself and, with the French, form a new line. That was two days before the first men began to return in the greatest secrecy, and the new line was never formed.

It was in Ramsgate that we first had real news of the return of men of the B.E.F. The high winding streets overlooking the harbour were lined with people as though to witness a procession. Roads to the harbour were cordoned. I had come across from Dover because I had heard something was happening. Few people knew what it was about. Rumour said hospital ships were coming in. The story of Dunkirk had not yet broken. It was a military secret, but one soon to be shared by people of the south-east coast ports who saw the first returning men pass through their town. It was on this Monday 29 May in Ramsgate that I realised the truth about the position of the B.E.F.

There were strange scenes and stranger stories in the Dover Grand Hotel, that week in May, the first after Trinity. Dunkirk was on, but not yet in full flood. Dover was still a busy untouched town. We were in the midst of history, not of it. Something was happening, something bigger than we knew. Sometimes a series of violent explosions would make the whole hotel quiver and set the seagulls screaming. It was the sound of the last fighting in Flanders.

Soon there was more than sound. George, the head waiter, was busy with the fish one night, and people were gossiping or drinking in the lounge or bar, when two or three naval officers came in. They were survivors from a lost destroyer. They were soaked from swimming in the sea and covered with oil. They were anxious for news of other survivors. One had his binoculars round his neck. Brushing by them were returned army officers with hollow eyes, sunken cheeks, unshaven. There were stories of men trying in desperation to stop German tanks with revolver shots, of refugees suddenly drawing arms from a handcart and opening fire, of German tanks being directed to secret underground petrol tanks hidden in a wood. Some had come from Calais. We became conscious of being in the backwash of tremendous events. Calais had fallen! That was the whisper, and it came as one more shock in a week of shocks. The last rearguard —the Guards—had fought their hopeless fight to the last. Boulogne had been evacuated for some days. And here was the backwash of a despairing, puzzled army suddenly turning up in the lounge of a hotel running with peacetime normality and the war still far away. It was fantastic. Little groups of French officers, puzzled, talked with each other, lost in a swirl of events that had been too much for them. I do not think that they knew what it was all about. No one knew much, anyway. Baggage and kit rescued from the battlefield was strewn about the hall. Outside were a group of much-braided, medalled Belgian officers. A pilot turned up from somewhere in full flying kit, had a drink at the bar and disappeared. Those few days and nights were a frenzy of submerged excitement, doubt and wonder. The stories and whispers and rumours were tattered fragments of history handed out while still being made. Everyone now knew the danger of the B.E.F. Many thought, with reason, we would lose the greater part of our army in France, if not as casualties, at least as prisoners. There was no sign of the miracle of Dunkirk.

I gave the *Daily Herald* office hints of what was going on ;

2

maybe they knew more, but the story that our army was struggling and straggling home could not yet be written. There were only a few journalists in Dover at this time— Hilde Marchant and McNally for the *Daily Express*, Stuart Young for the *Daily Mail* and Ronald Camp of the *News Chronicle*. We had the threads of the biggest story of the war so far, but could do nothing about it. We knew the B.E.F. was coming home. How could we know how much of it would eventually come back?

On Thursday 30 May the London newspaper offices were privately informed by the Ministry of Information that the censors would be prepared to consider stories about the homecoming of the B.E.F. By then there was nothing we could tell the enemy that he did not know! Our army was on the coast, or trying to reach the coast, and fighting with its back to the sea. London told us, and how we Dover journalists wrote! We had one of those rare stories that the nation was waiting for. For a day or two we had seen and heard of the landing of thousands of men from overcrowded ships. Men in the last stages of exhaustion and hunger, but we were able to say their spirits were unbroken and their rifles were slung. Telephoning was an agony. The Services had practically a monopoly. Whitehall at that time was in a rare frenzy. I went to Canterbury, and dictated the story that told for the first time that many thousands of the B.E.F. men had been brought safely home.

It was arranged by the War Office that next day, 31 May, facilities would be available for the accredited War Correspondents to visit Dover's piers and meet and talk to the men now coming home in their full flood of thousands. These War Correspondents were the uniformed men who had already been out in France and returned some weeks earlier. F. G. H. Salusbury, our own man, was, I think, still with the French forces. After some discussion concerning the lack of uniform, I was deputed to join the party.

The War Correspondents travelling from London overnight did not know that the cream of the story had been stolen by the ordinary staff reporters.

At 4 a.m. we had a telephone call from the military headquarters in Dover to report there immediately, the B.B.C. man, Bernard Stubbs,[1] who had arrived, and myself.

Hastily dressing, we drove to the pier, met the official War Office party and collected our armlets—since the War Correspondents were in uniform. But they had a great shock later when the morning papers came out with fairly full accounts of the gradual safe returning of the B.E.F. For all practical purposes the story had been told. It was, as someone remarked, a " triumph for the little men of Fleet Street ". We had worked for days, gleaning facts here and there, snatching a few hasty unofficial interviews with returned officers and men and generally getting a pretty good background to the situation.

We had seen very little, except as men marched to trains, but it was enough. That morning the newspapers had our report that many thousands of men from the B.E.F. had been brought safely out of Northern France and Belgium, when it had seemed that most would be lost.

Some of the War Correspondents were most annoyed at having the story stolen. They had no idea of the censors' relenting decision when they left London overnight. It was just one of those, to us, fortunate happenings. It was still more fortunate that I was able to carry on my preliminary unofficial work.

Actually most of our War Correspondents returned to London that day, but I haunted the pier for more than a week, until the first great flood of men became a trickle of last-minute stragglers and then died away altogether.

[1] *Bernard Stubbs went down in H.M.S. " Hood."*

CHAPTER TWO

THE MEN WHO CAME HOME

IF Dunkirk was not a victory for British arms, it was a mighty triumph for men of the B.E.F. These were the Cockneys, the suburbanites, the men of the shires, men from Scotland and Wales, who came home in their many weary thousands. That many came home at all was due to their grit and determination, and the unwavering leadership of their officers and N.C.O.'s.

In spirit they were unbeaten, and as I saw them, completely unbeatable. They were not lusty professional warriors, they were not the Guards, who, after days of bitter fighting, were later to put up their magnificent and traditional parade ground show on this Dover quayside. They were the Millwall football crowd, the men of Old Trafford and Roker Park, the men who stand round the Oval. The little ordinary men from a hundred trades, who lean over a garden fence to borrow a mower and chat for half an hour in doing it. The men who rush for the 8.45 or cram the early buses and take the dog for a walk on Sunday. Just the ordinary men of the street, of town and village. There were the Britishers who astonished the world and themselves and made us poor spectators stand for days with wonder in our eyes and hearts.

Some had fought bitter rearguard actions of a week or more before spending four or five days on the blasted beaches of Dunkirk and La Panne.

The first men I saw at close quarters came ashore from a crowded destroyer, a lean grey vessel and the first to slip through the haze that morning. As they came alongside they got busy with quips and cracks. "Put my name in the paper, guv'nor"—"'Oo says a Continental holiday"—"How's the beer"—"Nice day for a sail", and that sort of thing. Only when they stepped ashore did you realise their plight, and see their utter exhaustion of mind and body.

Some were bent with fatigue. Other men collapsed when their swollen feet left the gangway. Some were dizzy from exhaustion and it was cruel to try and talk to them. They could not understand. Tormented by constant bombing, weak from lack of food, the effects of every hard struggled mile were clearly marked. Yet a day or two later, at rest camps, these same men were fit and well.

This, again, is not an account of Dunkirk. It is just the angle I saw, my personal experience with the men, who, with the help of the Royal Navy and the Royal Air Force, had done the impossible.

Not that there were any thanks for the R.A.F. when our troops first landed. They thought the R.A.F. had let them down and did not then understand why it was they were safely there in packed thousands with no Nazi dive-bombers streaking out of the clouds. It makes me shudder now to think what the effects of dive-bombing on that congested Dover Harbour might have been, with ships of every kind berthed eight deep and some laden with troops almost to the water-line.

There were cries of "Where's the R.A.F." and facetious cheers if a single R.A.F. man was seen. It was understandable. The men had been heavily bombed on the way to the beaches, while they were waiting to be taken off and often after leaving. But the fact that more than 300,000 men were finally brought home to safety when it was once thought all would be lost is proof that the R.A.F. at Dunkirk did more than enough to hold the *Luftwaffe* off, as they did once again in Dover a few months later.

I talked to hundreds of men in that Dunkirk week and the general feeling was that someone, somewhere, somehow, had let them down. They could not yet grasp the course of the war. France had not yet collapsed and these men of ours came back a little puzzled and a little disappointed.

" I went out to fight, not bloody well come home," roared one terrific veteran sergeant as he walked down the gangway, rather as though he had been to a football match abandoned because of fog, and had not been given his money back.

It was a wondrous tragic sight, this home-coming of an army that through no fault of its own never had a chance to fight on equal terms. But where this had been possible, it was shown that, man for man, our troops were superior to the enemy.

The military history of Dunkirk must wait. My own feeling is, after meeting and talking with many of the men, that the B.E.F. went out to France rather expecting to begin where the trench warfare of the 1918 men left off. The army was not then ' Wavell conscious '. Even if a real opportunity for a counter-thrust had arisen, I doubt whether at that time we had the mechanised units to cope with the fast-moving German forces.

Disappointed or not, the B.E.F. came back from Dunkirk unbeaten in spirit, because, except for those desperate rearguard actions against heavy odds, which will remain some of the most glorious in history, they had had no chance to attack. But thousands had to fight their way to the coast and continue fighting almost to the point of embarking.

A typical journey was that described to me by a major :

" Our ship was shelled while we were loading and while proceeding to sea. We were bombed from the air and attacked by submarine—but we got through. This was possible because the fire of our warships and the attacks of our aeroplanes subdued the efforts of the enemy. Warships bombarded the German lines and fighters attacked the bombers. Before we reached the sea, German spies of every kind added to the difficulties. They directed the fire of German guns and the bombs of Nazi planes on our men."

One man said, " When we finally reached the coast and embarked, Germans were close behind us and a British warship turned back and fired on them before escorting us away. We found the strength to cheer because we saw the Germans were getting pretty average hell."

In Dover, women out shopping came across parties of Royal Marines and Royal Navy men bearing unmistakable signs of battle. Some wore captured German helmets while shopping in multiple stores. Some were wearing tennis shoes and odd clothes. They would have a drink or a shave and be on their way back to more fighting within an hour. I saw men come ashore covered with oil and water, have a bath, and go to sea again.

An officer came into the hotel after his ship had been lost. A few nights later he came in again. His new ship had been lost. A little later he had fixed up to serve in a third.

Many wounded were brought ashore and some were in a grievous state. Dover medical authorities had already been warned that an attempt was being made to evacuate as many of the B.E.F. as possible. But no one during the first day or two dreamed of a 300,000 figure. But large numbers of military casualties were expected and every doctor and nurse was mobilised. It was days before many went to bed. Doctors gave hundreds of anæsthetics during the five peak days, until in the end they were working automatically and all but asleep on their feet. There were all kinds of wounds to be treated. Some were machine-gun bullet wounds sustained on ships, some were from bomb fragments, some were burns caused by burst steampipes, fire and bomb damage. There were men with wounds sustained while fighting their way to the coast that had not been treated for a week. They had had no chance of getting in touch with a dressing station and the wounds were maggotty and festered. It was part of the treatment of this type of wound to leave the maggots until they had eaten the dead tissue. I give this unpleasant detail to indicate some of the hardships our men went through and conquered.

A happier story concerns a seven-years-old English girl, who had become separated from her English parents living in France, during the fighting. She attached herself to a party of Tommies and travelled with them forty miles. She walked part of the way and was partly carried, but mostly she had to walk because many of the men were in no condition to carry a baby, let alone a girl of seven. This little heroine, whose name I never heard, was embarked in a destroyer and brought to Dover. She was taken to hospital completely exhausted, the soles of her shoes worn right through. She was put into a warm bed and after she fell asleep nothing waked her. There was a heavy ' ack-ack ' barrage that night over Dover, but little seven-years-old slept on. Doctors were waiting to see her in the morning for they feared the experience might have left her seriously ill. They found her instead standing up at the end of her bed, singing childish songs to the soldiers.

I thought of another child that week. One of the thousands of men disembarking from a destroyer carried over his shoulder a cottonette container, rather like a Christmas stocking, filled with a few cheap toys. There was a trumpet sticking out, a small wooden horse and odds and ends like that. Heaven knows where the man had bought it and heaven knows how he kept it with him through those days and nights on Dunkirk beach. I talked to him, but he too was dazed with exhaustion, but his little gift of toys was securely fastened to his equipment. I turned away thinking that somewhere was a lucky child. We had no need to worry, I thought, with men like that.

Many men even brought back dogs with them. Not an odd dog here and there, not a dozen or so, but hundreds. I think the final figure was eight hundred. Every morning the whole length of that long Dover pier, strewn with the wreckage of battle, blood-stained equipment, men on stretchers or lying in weary groups, was the playground of dogs. Such odd dogs. There were large dogs, small dogs. They were all colours, black, brown, grey, white, and every shade between, and dogs with absurd tails. It was like a Cruft's dog show gone mad. It was the strangest medley of odd little dogs ever brought together. Every ship that came in had men on it with dogs in their arms, or led on a piece of string. You know what dogs are for attaching themselves to soldiers, and the sentimental heart of the British Tommy will never drive away a dog. These dogs were the forgotten strays of many an empty evacuated French village. It was a pity, but I am afraid most of them had to be destroyed. The local R.S.P.C.A. Inspector rounded them up by the dozen every morning. Some slipped out of the dock gates into the town, and I'll wager there are some French dogs in Dover to-day, probably attached to some troops. The affair of the dogs was one of the strangest side incidents in the whole of the Dunkirk week. It showed the heart of these men, like the fact that some of them had even managed to kick a football about on the beach near Dunkirk. At least they did, until deciding that having to continuously drop flat to avoid bombs interrupted the game to an impossible degree.

Nevertheless, there is no doubt that the constant and continuous bombing had badly shaken the nerves of some of the men. Having seen quite a lot of dive-bombing at close quarters, without being the direct objective, I can well believe it. It needs the strongest of nerves and the backing of adequate arms to face dive-bombing calmly. These men met it as their first experience of modern warfare. At the time the wounded were in hospital there were regular air-raid alarms in Dover and each alarm produced a tremendous effect on these men. Nurses often had difficulty in making them stay in bed while a raid was on, but after a day or two they recovered their normal cheerfulness. This concentrated experience of dive-bombing accounted for the widespread fallacy that the R.A.F. was not doing its part. "Thank God for the British Navy" was a remark always heard, but the plain truth is of course that but for the R.A.F. very few men would have got away at all.

The medical work carried on at Dover hospitals during this period was tremendous. Wall's ice-cream tricycles were even used to preserve blood transfusion banks.

One of the many heroes of this period was the matron at Union Road Hospital, Nurse Otterburn. She appeared to be a frail little woman, rather pale, with fair hair. She was running about morning, noon, and night and never appeared to tire, even at a time when the nerves of old friends and colleagues were so frayed they nearly came to blows. Nurse Otterburn always looked spruce and spry, as, indeed, did most of the nurses. They were worked to death, and later a detachment of Guy's Hospital nurses were sent down to relieve the strain. They were grim days, for in all some 6000 wounded were landed. After the first day or two many were taken away in hospital trains. Some men made the journey home and never survived this ordeal.

The whole town of Dover contributed something to the success of Dunkirk. The Southern Railway staff was tremendous. On peak days, when 60,000 were being taken off, trains crammed to the doors left the harbour station every few minutes. Tourist agency officials, used to handling Bank Holiday Continental crowds, helped in the work of despatch, and never was work done better than in getting these men away. Nearly 800 special trains were run by the S.R.

There was a great deal more in the organisation of Dunkirk than just bringing the men home. The ships had to run the gauntlet of every kind of attack, but at the same time had to find the way to take across necessary stores and food to Dunkirk for the tens of thousands of exhausted men still waiting on the beaches. Food and water and medical attention had been scarce. The Navy made it possible for 50,000 rations of biscuits, bully beef, chocolate, cigarettes and matches, and, above all, of water to be taken across. The most important need was for water.

It may be worth while to recall some of the stories of dogged heroism that I reported at the time. Sometimes men had been so exhausted after four days' forced marching and fighting that they collapsed on the sands and had to be half carried and half dragged to the boats by stronger comrades. In the last few days, too, the British soldiers suffered shelling as well as bombing, as the German forces drew nearer. Their only shelter was what they could scrape in the sand. One party of men forced their spirit to make them cover fifty miles in three days, and you can think for yourself what that means.

One major collapsed as soon as he stepped on Dover quayside and was taken away on a stretcher. His men described his superhuman endurance during four terrible days and nights, but he kept on his feet until the last step. Some men slept standing, as they were packed back to back in the overcrowded ships.

One man said, " We were bombed out of everywhere. I went to Armentières but it has been damaged much more than in the last war. We found spies everywhere and we could never stay more than one night in one place without being bombed to blazes by the German machines that came down like flies. It is quite true that the Germans have been systematically bombing and machine-gunning refugees. This is not a war, it is murder."

I was told too the story of a London bank clerk lieutenant who was killed the first time he met the enemy and was recommended for a posthumous decoration. It was on the Albert Canal, where he led an attack against a German pontoon landing party. Twice he returned for ammunition under heavy fire and the enemy was beaten back. He was killed by a bullet in the final exchanges.

At a casualty clearing station a medical officer absolutely opposed the suggestion that wounded would have to be left as prisoners. He got them away a few minutes before the Germans appeared.

A team of gunners held a bridge for twelve hours against overwhelming German forces. When the gunners finally had to retreat they left German corpses piled high.

The actual evacuation by sea gained the public limelight. Yet the scores of desperate rearguard actions that were fought before undoubtedly held up the Nazi advance long enough to give our men a chance to be taken off.

There was death, and little time for sentiment, but hardened doctors had to pause and think after the death of one naval officer. He had been shot through the eyes. When they went through his clothing, blood-stained and stenchy, they found a portrait of his wife. It was a portrait of such radiant happiness, one of those pictures that sometimes catches an expression that lives, that I think the doctors were sorry that they saw it.

I remember the morning when survivors of a Guards regiment, who had been engaged in heavy fighting along the Albert Canal came home, bearded, blackened and exhausted.

They lined up smartly and marched down the quay in

meticulously dressed threes. It was magnificent. It was the Guards.

At the station I saw on neighbouring lines trains containing men of the B.E.F. almost asleep from exhaustion and children who were being evacuated. Someone began to sing *There'll always be an England*. The words were taken up from coach to coach and the chorus was swelled to nearly a thousand voices as the children and the officials on the platform joined in.

Dover that week was no place for the sentimentalist. Yet the scene could not have produced in the heart of any even a tinge of the old-time ' glory of war ' nonsense. Rather it produced despair that British soldiers should have to put up with so much, that the strength of such hearts should be used to such little profit. Sweet-shops were crowded with children buying twopenny packets of chocolate to be given away—not eaten by the buyer. Now and again a man—at one place it was the station-master—would empty his hat full of coppers on the counter and distribute chocolate to outstretched khaki hands.

One of the best and most complete summaries I have heard of Dunkirk was given me by Vice-Admiral Sir Bertram Ramsay, who controlled the operation and was knighted for his work. This is an extract from his statement, which took nearly two hours to deliver. He spoke slowly, without a note, and seemed to have every detail in his mind. The room from which he and his staff had worked was called " Dynamo " because of the high-pressure work that went on day and night for ten days. The admiral said, and I quote the interview as it appeared in the *Daily Herald* because the statement forms a part of history :

" The room was supplied with seven telephones and staffed by sixteen men. You never heard such a hubbub. At the end of the whole nine days the officers who had been helping me said : ' It's been a hell of a time, but we really quite enjoyed it '. After three or four days the men working in the ' Dynamo Room ' were so tired that they were just lying down behind their chairs and falling asleep. As they woke up they would carry on with the work.

" In the first place 20 naval officers and 180 bluejackets were sent to Dunkirk to help in the later embarkation of 250,000 men at a place never intended for a ship. They were bombed all the way.

" The enemy decided that we should not be allowed to evacuate these armies and sent over hordes of bombers— hundreds. They made Dunkirk docks a shambles. The whole place was on fire and the heat was so great that no troops could come down to the docks.

" We had to make alternative arrangements or we could not get any men off. The only part of Dunkirk harbour where a ship could go alongside was a narrow pier of wooden piles, never intended for a ship to go alongside. There were no gangways and mess tables were put across planks.

" At the same time it became obvious that we must embark also from the beaches. We used a stretch of beach extending eight or nine miles from Dunkirk to La Panne. You could hardly find a more difficult beach for such a job. The distance from high-water mark to the nearest point where ships could lie was anything from half to three-quarters of a mile.

" After a couple of days all our landing parties were exhausted. They had had no sleep and every day we had to draw on another hundred men and, if possible, fifty more ships. Yet the cry was continually for more men and more boats, although we had denuded harbours at home of cutters, whalers and skiffs.

" About 29–30 May we were getting men away in better numbers than had been thought possible, rising from

15,000 the first night to 20,000 and 45,000 the second and third. We began to think we might do a big thing, so we asked the Admiralty to gather every single craft possible within twenty-four hours. The response was astonishing. Hordes of these little boats arrived. As the boats were sunk or abandoned the crews took to others. Nobody to this day knows quite what happened to anybody else.

" Our peak day was when 66,000 men were taken off, but that was only achieved at the expense of casualties to our boats.

" Several flotillas of destroyers were employed in this evacuation, but we never had more than twenty running at any one time.

" The Germans mounted heavy batteries commanding the direct route passing near Calais. We had to make a new route, which meant a round journey of 175 miles as against 76. That slowed us up, and then the Germans brought batteries commanding this route and we had to find a third, which had never before been used. This ran across sandbanks. It had to be buoyed and swept before we could use it.

" After this had been done the Germans brought up still more batteries.

" Daylight evacuation became impossible, and the rate dropped from 66,000 to 30,000 a day. But we went on to the end. Although no hospital ships came into this port more than 6000 wounded were landed from other vessels."

Before setting out on their last trip across the Channel men from British warships went round burning Dunkirk on commandeered bicycles to round up B.E.F. stragglers. They went round the blazing outskirts of the town crying " Any more for the old ' Skylark ', any more for a sail."

One of the last men I saw home was Sergeant J. Bull, of Hackney (" near the Wick "), who stepped ashore from a trawler. He was a member of an anti-tank unit which had been fighting the rearguard. His men gradually moved back from Brussels to Louvain and then to the coast. Finally they dug in with their guns on the sands of Dunkirk, covering the embarking men in case the German tanks broke through. Bull was the only British soldier in a boatload of French troops.

Many thousands of French troops were landed in the final days. Some of the Frenchmen carried thick staves cut from the countryside through which they had fought their way. I remember one man came ashore with a live goose under his arm. I saw a cat and a parrot as well. Another had a dog curled up asleep on top of his bulky pack.

The last Dover saw of the evacuation of the Channel ports were the columns of smoke pouring across the Straits from the blazing harbour buildings. One column of smoke, apparently from burning oil, drifted twenty miles down Channel. At night, from Shakespeare Cliff (which later, when Dunkirk had led to the Battle of Britain, became a grand stand for scores of correspondents and photographers), one could see a whole series of great fires raging along the coast. It was the end.

Dunkirk was a nine-days miracle and many of the best stories of the period may never be known. Most men trudged, hacked and fought their way back to the coast in small units. Many never knew where they had been. It seemed there had been complete confusion, following the break-through at Sedan, till the last man from Dunkirk had reached Dover and the smoke drifted silently over the sunny waters.

CHAPTER THREE

THE CHILDREN WHO WENT AWAY

After Dunkirk, Dover had a breathing space to consider its domestic affairs, and one of the first of these was the evacuation of the Dover children, or at least a sensible majority of them.

One of these rather sad days was Sunday 2 June. Many men from Dunkirk were still arriving, but the peak had been passed and it was time for the children to leave.

I was at the station that Sunday morning when the columns of marching children began to arrive. There were no crowds to see them off, no weeping mothers to make the parting harder. Approach to the station was closed, but even on the fringes there were very few parents and relatives. It was Dover's way of doing it, and maybe other towns in danger areas have followed the same practice. But in some areas there have been distressing farewell scenes at the station as the children have gone away, usually for the first time in their lives. At Dover all the last kisses and final admonishments were got through at the points of assembly. Then the parents returned home and the children set off. By the time they reached the station they had almost forgotten the parting and were ready to look forward to the adventures of the journey.

The children of the town seemed steadfast. They marched along in fine order, with never a tear among them, and entrained like young soldiers. I thought at the time that these children set a high standard, perhaps because as a garrison town Dover has always had a good sprinkling of regular troops, as well as a fine background of sea service.

Dover's salvage tugs and their accomplishments are famous. Besides, everyone remembers the smartness of the youngsters that used to attend the Duke of York's school near the town, before they were evacuated.

I have often thought that a very interesting section of the history of this war will one day be centred round the letters sent home by evacuees. It will be worth someone's while to collect these fragments of a nation's war history. To many of us one of the greatest burdens of the war lay in the sudden disruption of our home life. I wonder how many times separated husbands have said to themselves that after the war they will always " go home early " ?

I am reminded of all this by two recent letters received from my own small boy whom I have not seen for so many months. He writes, and I feel it is typical of thousands of scrawled little notes received in thousands of lonely homes every day :

" DEAR DADDY,—Last Monday I went to school. It was a good job I only took half my marbles with me or I would be bust because I lost that half. But I still have the ones at home.

" I take up the paper *Adventure* every week. It has a super story in it called Blood brothers of the homeless region. It is all about a gang of British spies in Germany. There is a town called Bellevue on the outskirts of Calais where some German people called oflag 47 have English slaves who are forced to dig a tunnel under the Channel. How would you like to see Germans coming up from an underground tunnel.

" We played Sticklepath on Saturday. I was not there to see it. When are you going to come and see me. A boy must see his Daddy sometimes.—From your loving son,

" CHRISTOPHER."

Well, despite the obvious confusion concerning the

activities of the Blood brothers, this is no doubt a typical letter.

Like my own boy, most Dover children went away. But one of Dover's greatest problems was what to do with the one thousand five hundred children, many of school age, who either remained in the town or have drifted back since danger began to seem less apparent. These children are of all ages, from babies and tots to boys and girls who should be at school, irrespective of any question of danger, yet are in a place where danger is liable to come at any moment.

You never know in Dover when something is going to happen, at any moment of the day or night. It may be only half a dozen shells or a few odd bombs, but it means the people live in a state of almost continuous Alert.

Right from the noisiest days of all, doctors have found that this state of affairs did not produce war neuroses. It has since been shown that as blitzes have spread to other towns there has been the same marked absence of apparent nervous effect. Arrangements made for treating cases of ' shell shock ' have scarcely been needed. The effect has often been the opposite. Doctors have told me that their usual number of ' nerve ' patients has fallen off considerably and they get fewer cases of people asking for a " bottle of something for my nerves ". Various reasons account for this. One is that too many people are busy with war work to worry about such things. Another is that the excitement of the moment tends to kill the strain on the nervous system. It does not necessarily mean that the human system is proof against abnormal shocks such as the sound of shells, bombs and every conceivable kind of gunfire. Some medical authorities take the view that any damage to the nervous system caused in this way will come out after the war. But it is looking too far ahead to try and forecast what people's reactions will be when peace comes.

I have seen some amazing examples of stolidity. I have seen groups of women standing chatting volubly on the pavement about some domestic matter with a clatter of gunfire going on not far away and perhaps a dogfight overhead as well. I remember watching once, with amused interest, a bowler-hatted gentleman going home from his office. He had umbrella and attaché-case and newspaper tucked under his arm, a typical ' City ' man. There was a tremendous to-do overhead at the time, but he just walked on with steady purposeful steps, apparently determined to ignore the whole business. I have seen old salts taking their usual morning doze in a seafront shelter, taking not the slightest interest in air battles. Not that the authorities want the old people and children here at all. Some of the old people, I am afraid, are stubborn to the point of stupidity. But it is even worse for children to be exposed. There may in certain cases be special reasons for keeping the children, but usually it is, at the very least, short-sighted selfishness. There will be serious regrets in a few years' time when parents begin to realise the harm they have done their children. There is definitely no merit in letting them remain unnecessarily in a dangerous place, and Dover was always dangerous.

One of the things I feel most strongly about is the question of the children's education. Without education, only too many thousands of our children will not be equipped to face the post-war struggles. This is not a peculiarly local problem, but it is worse in Dover than in London and elsewhere because there are no schools open at all. To open them, the authorities argue, would be to induce a steady trickle back of children already happily evacuated. It is, as I see it, one of Dover's biggest problems. Sometimes parents make the fatuous excuse " if we are going to die, we would rather all die together ". I doubt if the children would approve that view if they could understand the question. Already juvenile crime is increasing. We have had cases of young children in court for petty pilfering offences, and it is obvious that one of the problems we are merely playing with is that of the ' Dead End Kids '. Some Dover people took exception to that description, but it is true. Where children's parents will not act themselves the action should be taken for them. This is more important than closing the Sunday theatres, which Parliament has just solemnly voted. I am afraid this reads like a sermon, but the facts are there. At this very moment the Raiders Passed is sounding and anti-aircraft guns are going off at the same time.

It has frequently happened that bombs have fallen immediately after the Raiders Passed signal because, with the best warning organisation in the world—and at Dover it is very good indeed—it is impossible to keep trace of enemy raiders that are only five minutes' flight away. We are indeed a frontier town, a front-line position separated from the enemy by a No-Man's-Land that happens in this case to be the Straits of Dover. And therefore, though Dover did not seem the same without its bright children, I was glad that the majority had gone during early June, and sorry that any of them had stayed.

CHAPTER FOUR

EVERYDAY LIFE IN DOVER

By the first week in June the last stragglers from Dunkirk had trickled home, and by the end of the month Northern France was in German hands.

Dover had yet to experience bombing. Life in the town was normal. You could sit safely on the shingle by going through a gap left in the barbed wire. But the menace of Nazi troops and the *Luftwaffe* some twenty odd miles away had been brought much nearer.

Most of the correspondents went back to London after Dunkirk. I suggested I should do the same. There seemed no good reason to stay. But by now the London office had recognised that Dover was a key centre, and I began to feel that I might be there for the duration.

It was June, warm and peaceful. The open-air bath at Folkestone was an attraction. Heaven knows why, but no one seemed to realise we were standing on the end of a lighted fuse. The Grand Hotel resumed its normal functioning, catering for naval and military officers and a few civilians. The clamour of war had died away. No one seemed to have thought of the possibility of shelling from the French coast, or foresee that the next big enemy onslaught would be from the air.

Dunkirk appeared a disaster retrieved. After all, it was argued, we could refit and send out another B.E.F. France was still in the war—then. In fact, in those complacent days we still did not recognise the menace of the *Luftwaffe* over land and sea which would bring us to the risk of invasion.

Two or three weeks dragged by with desultory air raids and battles, but it was not until July that the first bombs were dropped on Dover. The pace was quickening. Soon Dover was to be world news.

At this time, early in July, we were still rather siren conscious. We were only on about the twentieth wail mark, and we still thought every Alert meant the immediate arrival of large numbers of enemy bombers, now known familiarly to Dover as ' they ' or ' nasties '.

Our raid psychology development followed along the lines of London and other towns before they were heavily bombed. In those days in Dover buses stopped running, some shops closed and hastily put their customers in the street. Now shop assistants say " And the next, please . . . a bit noisy, isn't it ? " The Post Office was one on the list of premises to close, and telephones went dead on the first note of the siren. This, of course, was in accordance with the extreme caution then advocated by officialdom.

I remember how the first air-raid warning of the war, on the Sunday when war was declared, produced the most marked reaction. I was at home near London that morning and thought, with everyone else, that it meant instant *Blitz*. I remember the heart-beating haste with which I got the car out and started to go to the office, thinking this was almost sure to be *It*. The warden at the end of my road was very excited, stopped my car, ordered instant cover in a nearby house and rushed on to hustle a cyclist off. We did not know so much about air raids then. I sneaked off a minute later and had difficulty in keeping going past wardens and police who had the official ' take cover ' policy well ingrained.

Everyone knows the history of air-raid sirens since, and how no one takes the slightest notice unless it seems that something is about to be dropped, and not always then.

In Dover, where for months there were anything up to a dozen Alerts a day, no other course is possible.

I think Dover's own war really started on Sunday 7 July. The entry in my diary for that day reads, " Biggest raid so far, when German machines attacked a convoy off Folkestone and our fighters engaged them over land. Terrific fighting, planes falling and machine-gunning all over the place. About 70 planes."

This raid produced the first air battles of the war over the Kent coast, and, so far as my experience went, some of the most dramatic of the many that followed.

It was just after dinner, though of course still daylight, when a series of terrific explosions were heard from sea. There was also considerable gunfire and machine-gunning. Two of us left to go to what is usually described as a ' cliff-top vantage point '—a part of a cliff outside the town some five hundred feet high. We had no steel helmets then, because the days when ' tin hats ' became a far more important part of our dress than umbrellas or mac-intoshes had not yet arrived. This attack was still some-thing new in our experience, though it was to mark the beginning of the *Luftwaffe* attempt to dominate the country in a matter of months.

Along the cliff edge was gathered a crowd of excited civilians, their cars parked by the side of the road. Over-head was being fought one of the most spectacular dog-fights I have ever seen—and since that day I have seen hundreds. There were some twenty machines in the fight, mostly *Messerschmitts*, which had engaged the few British fighters protecting the convoy, and the battle had swept on over land. It was the sort of battle no longer seen in 1941, with our regular Spitfire patrols in the air off our coast. They have changed the *Messerschmitt* pilot into a high-flying shy bird now ; he does not stay longer than he can help, and he shows a marked disinclination to

' mix it ' with our Spitfire patrols. On this Sunday evening
last July it was different, and the MEs' pilots were undoubtedly keen on carrying the battle over our own coast.
They still believed they were about to master our Fighter
Command. The combat too was fought out much lower
than has since become fashionable with new, faster and
high-flying machines. This fight was on at the height of
not much more than 10,000 feet. To-day they battle at
20,000, 25,000, 30,000, even 35,000 feet, sometimes completely out of sight.

These machines, British and German, could be clearly
followed as they circled round each other, looking for an
opening. Machine-gun fire was continuous, and we looked
up at the grim spectacle with eager fascination, quite
regardless of the thousands of spent bullets that were flying
about and were later picked up in fields and along the
cliffs. It was our first air battle, and we were not then so
expert at following the action as we have since become,
although the tactics of a large-scale air battle is always
difficult to understand. The swooping and diving seems
aimless until it becomes clear which two machines have
singled each other out as possible victims. One or two
machines close in, and as they pass machine-gun fire gives
its sinister rat-tat-tat. It does not need to be a long burst,
with Browning guns spitting their 9600 bullets a minute.
A firing burst of more than a few seconds from any one
machine is rare. If the pilot hits his target, a few seconds
are sufficient to bring his opponent crashing to sea or land.

So it was on this fine sunny Sunday evening, when many
of us at Dover saw sudden death for the first time. The
duel between the fighters seemed to have developed into
a general mêlée. Then two of them fastened alongside
each other for a second or two. They were quite low, and
we realised, unpleasantly, this was the kill. There was
a burst of machine-gun fire and a cigar-like glow appeared

in the body of the *Messerschmitt*. The glow spread to a flame and the machine rocketed to earth in a shroud of smoke and flame. The whole terrible drama lasted less than a minute. I have seen scores of machines, both enemy and British, destroyed since, but few incidents have given me such a shock as this first close-up view of death in the air. It seemed—and I still get the same feeling—rather indecent to stand lamely on the ground and gaze at the efforts of two men about to give and avoid death. For them, yes, it is war, they themselves would say it is their job. For us spectators it is a grim thrill, but there is nothing one can do but stand and watch. It is quite beyond the control of human expectancy not to do so.

The destruction of this Nazi was not the end of the battle, which continued for a few minutes longer. Then the sky cleared, the *Messerschmitts* vanished, and the Spitfires returned home.

But from this evening onwards, similar such air raids and air attacks became a continuous feature of the Dover life and the people quickly adapted themselves to it. Errand-boys began to go about with tin hats on the handle-bars of their machines. The man selling flowers from a stall in the Market Square had one handy. Many house-wives began to carry them and ' tin-hat time ' became a popular local expression.

Dover has never suffered such concentrated heavy bombing as Coventry, Cardiff, Bristol and other big cities, but it has had far more raids than any other town in the country. In Dover the bombs come in fewer numbers but fairly regularly, although in recent months it has been comparatively ' quiet '. And when there are no bombs there is always the possibility of a few shells lobbed across the Straits from Nazi guns.

This has created an impression that Dover is an unten-able shambles. But nothing could be farther from the truth. The town has suffered heavily, but the casual visitor coming from the station might at first see little amiss. He would see gaps here and there and notice the absence of glass in the shop windows down the main streets, but only in certain areas near to the sea front would he find real blitz effects. Apart from these bad areas, damage throughout the town is spasmodic, where odd bombs and shells have fallen. The impression that there is ' nothing left of Dover ' is quite wrong.

St. James' Church has had to be closed for the duration of the war as a result of damage by enemy action. The parish church of St. Mary's has suffered damage to its stained-glass window at the east end. Old St. James' Church has also been badly damaged. The adjoining hall, used for centuries when the Lord Warden opened his courts, was almost destroyed. St. Barnabas' Church was so badly damaged that its use has had to be abandoned. St. Paul's Roman Catholic Hall was almost destroyed and the Salvation Army Citadel rendered unusable.

The Masonic Hall, St. James' School, the Parish Hall, and the Swimming Baths have all been damaged.

Two of Dover's biggest hotels, the Grand and the Burlington, suffered severe damage. The Grand Hotel has been struck on several occasions. Then one day the tower of the Burlington Hotel received a direct hit. Other buildings badly damaged in the town at different times have included several garages, the covered market and scores of shops and houses. Many people have had their windows blown out half a dozen times. But for all that, the first casual impression of Dover is that suggestions of damage have been exaggerated. This is probably because air raids have been numerous but only rarely severe. Each report of shelling, too, has helped to create a picture of a battered town, hanging on to life in clouds of smoke and rubble. Nevertheless, though for military reasons it has not been possible to indicate where shells have fallen or what their apparent objective has been, for the comfort of people with friends or relatives in Dover I would say that that picture is not a true one. *The Front Line*, the film of how Dover carries on, is proof of the contrary.

I give these facts, not to minimise the damage done or underrate the pluck of the town-people who lived for months under continuous war conditions, but to show that in a bombed and shelled area some twenty miles from the enemy, life can and does go on much as usual. The real point about Dover's war life is the way it has carried on in the face of continued activity of one kind or another.

The Dover Hippodrome has given its twice-nightly variety shows almost continuously, and is one of the wonders of war-time amusement. It is one of the last privately owned theatres in the country. Through all the summer period of shells and bombs it continued with its twice-nightly show, except on a few occasions when it seemed too dangerous.

In the stage bar the audience can meet the artistes straight after their turn. Troops in steel helmets, with rifles, sailors straight from some dangerous job in the narrow Straits of Dover, come and exchange jokes with the comedians, dancers and singers. Usually the artistes are persuaded to give three or four shows a week to the Services, above their twice-nightly appearances.

Mr. Geoffrey Warner, the comedian compère, has organised many shows in trawlers, at remote batteries and camps in the district. Not long ago he and his wife were bombed, with other members of the company, when about to give a show. They had just arrived at the hall when a bomb dropped on the stage. The piano was dug out of the crater and carried to another building.

In less than an hour the party was giving a performance as promised. Several men had been injured and first aid was given by the pianist of the party, Mrs. Geoffrey Warner, formerly a nurse.

Before the war the Hippodrome was due for demolition and reconstruction. Now it is carrying on, and providing ' the stuff to give the troops '.

The *Dover Express* has come out every week, despite difficulties caused at times by ' enemy action '. It has frequently and severely and sometimes unjustly criticised the efforts of London and American correspondents, but the right spirit has been there. I somehow feel that if ever enemy troops occupied Dover, the veteran editor, Mr. Bavington Jones, would come out with some caustic comments regarding their habits, manners and customs. Mr. Jones, aged about sixty, with a grey moustache, was a Chief Warden until a severe illness caused him to give up. A Storm Trooper, I am sure, would get as much change out of Mr. Jones as does the local council, when he thinks they are not following the right path.

How well the *Dover Express* reflects the spirit of the town and people may perhaps be gathered from a newspaper impression from far away—from the *Newark Evening News*, New Jersey, in the United States. Here is the extract :

" *The Dover Express*

" The streets, as well as the Straits, have their tales of quiet courage, on which Hitler might reflect.

" *At dawn, fourscore German bombers and fighters rose from their fields in France and Belgium and made for the port and town of Dover, which lies across the narrow waters of the English Channel some nineteen miles from Calais. The 30 Junkers streamed down in almost vertical power dives in waves of eight, while 50 Messerschmitts fighters stood off the defending English Spitfires and Hurricanes. Terrific detona-*

tions shook houses along Dover's sea front, spouts of water shot a hundred feet in the air and showered ships at the docks. The ships tossed like corks in the churned water.

" When the Germans had departed, Dover extinguished its fires, removed its dead, cared for its wounded. The Dour, which breaches the high chalk cliffs on either hand, resumed its quiet seaward flow. The Roman lighthouse in Dover Castle still stood.

" Where once the wooden towers of Saxon Harold and Norman William defended this coast the ramparts were still intact. Dover resumed its business.

" What kind of business can Dover do under the lethal rain of such attacks ? What is the state of mind of its inhabitants ? Are those of its people who have not been evacuated still concerned with the routine of life ? Or are these German attacks, such as the one just described, which occurred earlier this week, shattering Dover's morale and spreading panic through its streets ?

" The writer has had the privilege of examining a recent issue of the Dover Express & East Kent News, one of those English provincial weeklies that reveal far more of the intimate spirit of England than the great London Dailies. This issue is less than a month old and was made available to The News through the kindness of Alexander Wadsworth of 162 South Eighth Street, Newark.

" Into Dover, a few weeks earlier, had streamed from Dunkirk and Calais the survivors from the Battle of Flanders. Ships and boats of all categories had landed their cargoes of troops at Dover, and returned to the French coast for more. Had Hitler gone to Calais he could have seen Dover through his field-glasses in clear weather. Dover, were it curious, could have seen the coast of France.

" Dover, however, was not bothering about Hitler or the coast of France, if the Dover Express reflects the preoccupations of its people. The Dover Express published an *editorial headed ' Nota Bene '. It stated that an English version of W.P.A. was at work in Dover and that the workers ought to have been with the troops.*

" *DOVER'S CONCERNS.*

" *Here are a few excerpts from this editorial.*

" ' *When the war is over there will come a reckoning time.*'

" ' *Dover is a safe place but it has been made a bankrupt town.*'

" ' *The Town Council have still time to act.*'

" ' *George Bernard Shaw is afraid that Bumbledom will win in the fight against Defence of the Realm.*'

" ' *It is a danger. Bumbledom is responsible for Dover to-day being engaged in building an Infants' School and laying water mains. The workers on all such jobs should have been transferred to work in preparing to resist invasion.*'

" ' *The Maginot Line, which most of us believed was far more extensive, might have been lengthened considerably.*'

" ' *All over Kent Bumbledom has kept workers busy on Parish Pump jobs, whilst the Empire has received savage blows from the Nazi Hun.*'

" ' *Had such workers been transferred to France months ago, the German tanks might have been stopped by tank traps.*'

" ' *When will the Town Council take action ?* '

" *What action the Town Council took is not apparent, but at all events the Town Council was much occupied with other vital concerns. On a suggestion from London, a resolution was presented to reduce the Town Council to nine members, in case of evacuation or other crisis in the affairs of Dover. The Mayor explained that London wanted an evacuation of ninety per cent. The Council rose in its wrath at the mere idea. Councillor Walker enquired, with withering sarcasm, how he could go inland and float his boats.*"

(Councillor J. G. Walker was later killed by enemy action while in the very act of attending his boats on the beach. At that time Dover seafront was not a very healthy place, but although he could not put to sea, Mr. Walker, fifty-four years of age, spent an hour or so every day pottering about with his little craft.)

" ' *The evacuation discussion continued*', *wrote Mr. Suydam. The Mayor answered Councillor Walker by saying that London wanted all possible persons to get out.*

" *Councillor Walker repeated that he did not want to go out of the town. Why should he? It was ridiculous. What was he to do—be sent somewhere foreign? It was all well enough to send people rushing about, but when people were concentrated in one place the same thing would happen again. England was, after all, an island. There were limits.*

" *There were limits to the Mayor's patience too, as the following exchange took place and will show :*

" ' THE MAYOR : *Do you take me for a liar, or what ?*

" ' ALDERMAN POWELL : *I beg your pardon. No ! I took you for a gentleman, which you are.*

" ' THE MAYOR : *I have tried to be all the time I have been on this Council.*

" ' ALDERMAN POWELL : *Do not lose your temper. If you lose your temper you lose the battle.*

" ' THE MAYOR : *I can fight my battles without your assistance. Everyone is a damned liar except you.*

" ' ALDERMAN POWELL : *Oh no, please do not talk like that, Mr. Mayor, it is not nice.*

" ' COUNCILLOR AUSTEN : *Tell the Regional Commissioner that one hundred per cent. of the Council will stay and that we shall not desert the town. London has no authority to tell us what to do.*'

" *One of the women members remarked that Dover was her home, she had no other place to go and she would remain. The still obstreperous Councillor Walker said it would have a big effect through the Empire ' if the Dover Town Council is going to remain 100 per cent.'. He moved that it should remain so. The Mayor then formed a motion to take no action to form a council of nine, and it was carried 10-3.*

" Come on, Stukas and Junkers, dive on Dover and drop your bombs, but the Dover Town Council isn't going to desert the town. You can't drive these people out, mein Fuehrer, at least not with bombs. Armies and tanks might do it, but while your machine-guns rattle on the roof tiles, B Company, Green Howard Regiment, advertise themselves as ' in want of a pianoforte to liven up their evenings off duty '. A lance-corporal has been married in the parish church and the brides-maids wore ' silver Juliet caps and carried posies of sweet-peas '.

" The Archbishop of Canterbury preached on Sunday morning and was received at the door with a guard of honour from the Buffs.

" Yes, life goes on in Dover, at least it was going on three weeks ago, and there's not much reason to suppose it isn't going on there now. The first page of our Dover Express, *according to usual English newspaper practice, consists of birth, marriage and death notices, together with ' prepaid advertisements '— what would be classified advertisements in the United States.*

" Here one gets brief impressions of how life begins, continues and ceases in this small English town, with the war receiving no more than an occasional passing reference.

" In the birth column, Mr. and Mrs. —— announce ' the gift of a daughter '. Another couple announce the birth of ' a brother for Esme '. There is an announcement of a silver wedding—married at Dover in 1915 and still living there. There is a paragraph headed ' killed in action ', wherein is set down the death, in June 1940, of a Warrant Officer on H.M.S. ' Glorious '—' in loving memory of Charles ' is the reserved reference of his parents to their one son, now gone. A little further down the column someone wants an ' experienced general

4

maid, modern house, liberal outings'.   London needs pro-
bationer nurses for Tooting Bec hospital.   Wiltshire wants a
first grocer's assistant ' for the duration '.   Someone wants
a cook, ' wages £1 a week : no entertaining '.

  " An engraver offers ' identification bracelets, engraved,
complete, 2s. 6d. each, post free.'   Someone else wants to sell
a ' full-sized drum set in good condition, £3."   There is a
series of startling paragraphs, somewhat as follows :

  " ' Guns !   Guns !   Guns !—garden guns, sporting guns,
air guns.   Purchasers must be over seventeen years of age.'

  " ' Catapults !   Catapults !   Catapults !   Scout knives in
stock.'

  " ' Darts !   Darts !   Darts !   Darts and dartboards—
footballs—gloves.'

" ' GEORGE, SNARGATE ST., DOVER.'

  " Not to be outdone, Webber & Son, of 12 Castle St.,
Dover, make this simple announcement :
  " ' Arms.—We can still supply guns and cartridges for
bird-scaring.   Suitable musketry advice given.'

  " One advertiser wants to sell ' twelve unflighted canaries',
another a ' job lot of second-hand pianos '.   Still another
advises those who are leaving Dover to store their furniture
' in a nice dry store '.   Under ' Coming Events ' there is an
announcement that ' Old Contemptibles Association, Dover
Branch,' meets the first Friday in each month.   Could these
be the Old Contemptibles of the 1914 retreat from Mons ?
None other !   Oh, and there's dancing at Castle Hill House
twice a week, admission 1s. each, private lessons given.   The
gentleman with the unflighted canaries wants to sell them again
at the bottom of column 4, and the Town Council has ordered
hairdressers to close four times a week at 7 p.m.

  " As one folds the Dover Express *to put it aside, thinking*
one's own thoughts about this corner of England that is
closest to Hitler's armies, the black silhouettes of four German

aerial troop-carriers fix one's gaze. The War Office requests readers to cut them out, paste them on cardboard and hang them in their homes. Here is a Junkers 53, most often used for 'paratroop dropping', Junkers 86, Junkers 90 and Focke-Wulf 200 Condor.

" In the column beside these terrible outlines is a list of those who sent floral tributes to the funeral of a young girl, for in Dover it appears to be the custom to publish the cards attached to such floral remembrances. Here one finds Mum and Dad, Mrs. Clack, Fred and Flo, Tich Wraight, Mrs. Gotherage of Winchelsea ; Albert, Queenie, Beryl, Ada and Charlie, Nin and Violet. One wonders whether Mrs. Gotherage of Winchelsea, poring over her silhouettes, can spot the smooth stream-lined fuselage of a Focke-Wulf 200 Condor, or whether Queenie and Beryl will recognise on sight the leading edge of the wing of a Junkers 90, which has a very pronounced ' sweep-back '."

Perhaps Dover Council meetings are not always as flamboyant as the one reported here. But that the Council are very proud and independent I know, and its members have undoubtedly set a standard for the town.

Alderman J. R. Cairns, the Mayor, has described himself to me as a ' pig-headed old Geordie '. He is a red-faced man, with a good moustache, manager of a tarmac works, but now with the more important job of holding together the town during its most critical period.

Dover has a good background of war. In 1914–18 it was the first town to be bombed by the enemy, was shelled from the sea and its harbour was used by thousands of men proceeding on and returning from leave.

The Town Council quickly set the example, although it was not at first followed by other authorities. They decided to carry on their meetings through Alert periods, even though in those early days there was a general official tendency, in Dover as everywhere, to "close everything down". It seems strange now that buses once stopped running through Alerts, that the post office closed, telephones went dead (that took a long time to put right), shops hustled their customers into the streets and generally everyone did what the authorities had decided ought to be done during raids, quite regardless of the effect on trade and business.

So the Town Council decided to carry on and it is as well they did. Many times the wail of the siren has interrupted the meetings and members have had to wait for the long-drawn-out scream to die away before carrying on with their remarks, contentious or otherwise. Sometimes people in Dover are inclined to be critical because these die-hard Town Fathers take their duties very seriously. Yet for all the apparent irrelevance of some of their debates they are the men who have stood by the town and are seeing it through a difficult period, facing bankruptcy and bombs. Personally I have always found any kind of Council meeting a thing to be avoided at all costs, but I follow Dover's deliberations with interest, because they are part of history.

One day the Education Committee was discussing the vexed question of the evacuation of the children. It turned into a fast and furious debate, but some of the quieter members could hear bombs whistling down. One councillor indeed jumped up and said, "Bombs are falling," but no one else took the slightest notice of this interruption and went on with the discussion.

On another occasion a bomb fell on a nearby building during a Council meeting. There was a terrific bang and plaster began to fall from the ceiling of the Council chamber. Several councillors jumped up, but the Mayor said : "It's all right now, it's dropped", in his pawky Tyneside manner. Mayor Cairns in fact gives the impression that if his sergeant-at-arms came in and said, " Excuse me, the Germans are here," the Mayor would reply with righteous indignation, that a meeting of his Council could not be interrupted in that unseemly way, and would demand respect to the chair. Dover knows its place and is prepared to stick to it.

The traders of the town had a meeting during the *Blitz* period to decide at what time they should close. A shell dropped close by, shaking the building (and shells seem to carry a louder and more sustained blast than bombs), and the shelling warning was sounded. Other shells could be heard exploding, but the meeting went on and the business was carried through to its proper conclusion.

Another incident concerns a printer in the Home Guard. During one shelling his house was hit. He cleared up the mess as best he could and went on Home Guard duty.

Difficulties or not, Dover carried on.

Mr. F. C. Overton, who calls himself ' Dover Blitz teacher ', runs weekly dances in the Town Hall and finds plenty of men in the Services anxious to have their steps polished up, war or not. Only when he organised his annual dancing contest did the programme make a slight concession to the war. An amendment read, " Owing to prevailing war conditions and insurance cover, the Challenge Cups must be returned to the organiser at the conclusion of the dance to-night, in order that they may be placed in safety ". Dancing went on until midnight, which isn't bad, twenty miles from the Fatherland.

There is a dance of some sort every night in Dover, a private Services affair or a public dance. During the winter the Rugby Club began to open up again, and it was quite a usual sight to see its secretary scuttling round among the Services or anywhere else for possible Rugby players. The Yacht Club, on the battered sea-front, is still open, although yachting has long since ceased, and all its windows are broken. Yet it still forms a meeting-place for some of Dover's old members, who look over the war-tangled front and harbour, holding the fort until the young yachting members come back. The Conservative Club and the Oddfellows' Club are open, there is public snooker and billiards, for experts and rabbits alike.

There is a story about Mead, an old soldier and veteran steward of the Dover Club. A big bout of shelling had started just about lunch-time and the members retired to the cellar. This seemed temporarily to upset Mead's luncheon arrangements, which had never been upset before, so he rallied round in the best Jeeves style, obtained some corned beef and bread and took this down to the cellar with the intimation that lunch was served.

Almost every remaining able-bodied man in Dover has a war job of some kind. Dover's civil defence services are among the best organised in the country. They had their trials well before those of the other towns and carried on during all the shelling. One ambulance, for instance, had a shell very close to it during the first bombardment, and one of the crew was killed. Deverson, a popular local hairdresser, left his saloon one day to go on duty as usual during a raid and was killed when sheltering a woman from a bomb. The splinter that killed him went right through his steel helmet.

When the Catholic Church of St. Paul's was said to be unsafe, the Catholics of the town very soon got together and themselves repaired it. Volunteers cleared up the débris on the church floor, led by Father Oscar Leeke, who was himself injured by a splinter. Other people nailed boards to cover the blown-out windows.

One local butcher's counting-house assistant has the reputation of never having gone into an air-raid shelter. Once a warden popped his head in when the shelling was getting a bit rough and found her busy as usual with her books.

People whose work was cut short " as the result of enemy action " soon looked round to find other. Mr. S. L. Buxton, who was manager of a skating rink until it was wrecked, turned up again a little later managing a cinema. George, head waiter at the Grand, bald and beaky, who would be angry when you came in late for a meal and next moment challenge you to darts, found himself managing one of Dover's biggest bars.

I have found others of the staff now carrying on at the only other hotel in Dover—with the exception of private hotels. Many of the windows of this hotel have been broken from nearby bombs. A few naval officers are the only regular guests, and the staff go about their work with quiet efficiency. They are only young girls, like the one who made my bed when I stayed a few nights to write this story of Dover. She told me, brightly, she " didn't mind a bit ", and added, " there are a lot of people wouldn't come down to this town for anything, but I've been here all the time. A block of flats I was working in once was shelled just after I had left for a walk, but we went back later on and worked as usual. I don't mind a bit about things like that."

There are other girls here too from the bombed Grand Hotel who do not seem to mind in the slightest that they are in what is potentially one of the most dangerous spots in England.

I give these incidents, trifling though they may seem in themselves, to try and give a picture of everyday life in this peculiarly placed war town. It is an education to walk down Bench Street or one of the other main roads of Dover any sunny morning. It will seem crowded and animated—in fact in the spring of 1941 there was a distinct tendency at the moment for people to come back to Dover. At one time last summer the town's population was reduced. Now there are indications of a general drift back, a number of people having returned in recent months, and sun-bathing is popular again.

However, Bench Street on a fine sunny morning can look prosperous. The Creamery Café is crowded with people drinking coffee. Many of the girls are " Wrens ", who do all kinds of mysterious jobs for the Navy, from driving cars to decoding. They come in for morning coffee rather like girls at a university town and with them are Service people in general. It can sometimes seem very quiet and peaceful in the ' front line '.

In one of the more popular districts of the town Mr. F. A. Vickery pluckily carries on his damaged oyster bar. He had only been open a couple of months, sensing the possibility of building up a connection among troops and sailors, when a nearby bomb damaged his premises, smashed all his windows, as well as those of many other buildings in the district, including taverns and cafés, which he relied upon to bring trade to his oyster bar. Within a few weeks he opened up again, with wire-netting in place of windows, behind which he displayed his oysters and cockles, not to mention whelks. Now Mr. Vickery, a rather lugubrious-looking figure, stands in his doorway, gives a watery smile and assures you that business " isn't too bad, not too bad at all . . . but can't get the stuff, you know. . . ".

There are scores of examples like that in Dover, because the tradespeople have probably been hit harder than anybody else. In the months that I have been here I have seen a steady succession of shops and premises close down, some following bomb or shell damage, some simply because they could not make ends meet. There are scores of untold stories of the hardships of the little people, but those that remain take up the attitude " here we are and here we mean to stay. Jerry can't drive us away."

Very fine shelter accommodation throughout the town has helped to keep the casualties down to a comparatively low figure. Dover's great chalk cliffs form natural shelters, at one point running through half the main part of the town, and with accommodation if necessary for some 8000 people. Some people have made their homes in these caves ever since being bombed out of their own homes.

It seems strange now to reflect that in the early days of Dover's shelling and bombing we were saying " London must carry on like Dover ". We know now that there is no difference between the people of Dover and those in other towns. The only difference in Dover is that the hardships have been more numerous and varied, more continuous and sustained, although never on such a heavy scale as, for example, at Plymouth and Coventry. But we have *seen* more of war here than anywhere else.

Old Richard Chapman, " Dick ", carries on in peace and war as his father did before him. He holds one of the town's oldest offices—Town Sergeant—and carries the 1660 Mace before the Mayor. In peace-time he used to talk to visitors about the thirteenth-century Town Hall. Now he attends council meetings and the routine of generations is carried on, war or no war. He has been doing the job for thirty years, as his father Steven did for thirty-six years before him. Dick, one of the town's characters, is another of those people not to be put out by any Nazi.

Or take a look at " The Orange Tree ". The walls of this small resort of seamen and railway workers are lined with a series of some of the strongest, most biting and satirical cartoons I have seen. They are the work of a natural self-taught artist, Cyril Green, a thirty-two-year-old Southern Railway worker, now in the army. When in Dover he would do one or two cartoons a week, thinking out his own ideas, and in between sketched customers. He has never had any official recognition of his work or any special teaching, but his 'gallery' at "The Orange Tree" is one of the most remarkable I have ever seen.

Nearly everyone in Dover has felt the effects of the war in one way or another. The Mayor had a brother-in-law killed by a shell, and a number of Dover men have been lost on service at sea, particularly during the Dunkirk days.

The Chief Constable, Mr. Marshall H. Bolt, who received the O.B.E. at the New Year for war services in the town, has had his worries. But that does not prevent this cheerful red-faced bowler-hatted man from keeping a watch for fifth columnists—not that there is any reason to suppose there are any in Dover.

In a hairdresser's saloon in the main street "Polly", a twenty-nine-years-old South American parrot, is seeing this war through with the same ruffled indignation of the last. Then the bird used to make inelegant gestures when "Kaiser" was mentioned. Now he has developed the same trick with "Hitler", and it is much admired.

These may seem small-time home town details. But they give a picture how the English town nearest the enemy continues its life, without worrying overmuch, in the middle of a war in which the whole Empire is at stake.

I gave a short broadcast talk once on the people of Dover. The concluding words were, "the people of Dover are as solid as the cliffs around them". They still are.

CHAPTER FIVE

BRITISH SHIPS AND SAILORS

In July, as the German air offensive gathered increasing momentum, we saw our sailors in action and out of action, defying the Nazi dive-bombers, beating them off and carrying on.

Time and time again I have seen British seamen return from some inferno of bombs, met them the same evening and have been amazed by their spirit. I saw all over again the men of Dunkirk.

I used to call at one " Sailor Pub ", and there, more than anywhere, I found the spirit of Dunkirk and of the Dover Town Council. I have seen men come into it straight from wreck and carnage, from the ordeal imposed by continued dive-bombing and machine-gunning, and soon they would join in and be singing *Mother Machree* with the others. I met them every evening ; heard their stories and their songs. They were terrific.

One man came in with a big joke one night. He told us why he was so amused. A few hours before he had been lying flat on the deck of his ship while bombs burst all round it. " Suddenly," he said, " I felt a clump on the back of my neck—and there seemed to be so much blood about that I knew I was dying. But do you know what it was ? It was red ink from a stone bottle that had been blown out of the purser's office by the force of an exploding bomb." There were roars of laughter and the red ink joke lasted all night.

Another man in " Sailor Pub " had been less lucky in

a similar mishap. During a raid his ankle had been broken by a flying jar of pickles and he had just come out of hospital. " I wouldn't have minded if it had been a bomb splinter," he said, " but a jar of pickles . . . ! " The men off the bombed ships began to chip him all over again. It was another good joke.

One evening I saw a party of seamen brought into a sailors' hostel, all of them covered with oil and water, many of them covered with blood.

That same evening, in " Sailor Pub " (it has been bombed since, together with the hostel), I saw them after they had been rigged out in new suits from a local out-fitters. They were grouped round the piano, lustily singing *Rose of Tralee*, *Oh Johnny*, *Roll Out the Barrel*, and all the other favourite songs of war and peace. They looked like a party of workmates on a beanfeast, and no one could have guessed at their experience of a few hours before.

On another occasion an elderly seaman, aged about sixty, was brought ashore and sent to hospital with a severe arm wound. A rough tourniquet had been fixed by his shipmates, but when they left him at hospital they feared he would not live through the night. Next morning he was as bright and cheerful as ever and insisted on seeing the mate about signing on again.

A small collier had been struck by a bomb. Her gun fired as she was sinking—and in her final moments her gunner blew the wings off a *Dornier*. The men who escaped with their lives told me that story with pride. Anyone who could get a *Dornier* was envied in those days.

These same men told me that, while they were being bombed, they could see sailors on a nearby destroyer helping their own gunners by standing on the deck and firing rifles at the dive-bombers as they swooped down mast high. Many men have told me it is a great comfort on occasions such as this to be able to do something towards hitting back. Even a man who is able to do nothing more than fire a seemingly futile rifle feels far better for it.

Someone else told me the story of a diver who was at work when bombs began to fall. They sent a message down to him that bombers were ' about '. He sent back his reply—" What the hell's that got to do with me "—and went on with his job.

I took Vincent Sheean, the well-known author and journalist, into " Sailor Pub " one night. In the small back parlour a rather pretty young woman played the piano endlessly, tune after tune, song after song. She seemed to know them all. She would occasionally sip a glass of sherry and go on playing. If at times the words were a trifle irregular she did not turn a hair but just carried on. She was there from six until ten, doing her job, going quietly home and coming back next night. She was a most demure young woman, with her gloves and little attaché-case.

One night a hero of the " Graf Spee " action had turned up. He stirred the company to silence and cheers with his rendering of *Down Montevideo Way*—the story of the River Plate action set to the tune of *Down Mexico Way*—still one of the war's favourite songs.

One of the greatest successes as a singer I met at that time was one Stoker Stubbs. A tough-looking tubby little chap, he had the most tremendous voice and a large repertoire of sentimental songs. One night, in quite a large hall, he reduced a noisy crowd of soldiers, sailors, airmen and their friends to silence with *Trumpeter, What are You Sounding Now?* These men are sentimentalists at heart, and the sentiment of this, to its final echoing call, was a little too near reality for some of them.

The civilian population of Dover quickly caught the

spirit brought ashore by these seamen when they came into the town.

Take this incident. In the clouds circled a group of dark specks. The flash and crackle of machine-gun fire could be heard. A newsboy was looking up with interest. His comment was " I shouldn't be surprised if 'oastile aircraft ain't in the vicinity " with heavy but typical front-line humour. After that ' 'oastile aircraft ' became a popular local catch-phrase.

A doctor, whose house on the sea-front has since suffered from enemy action, coined the phrase " How's the Father-land to-day ? " as he strolled out to see how clearly the cliffs of France could be distinguished.

At that time the basement of his house was the refuge every hour or so of a girl who was continuing to sell ice-cream at a kiosk on the front. At least half a dozen times a day she had hurriedly to put up her shutters and make for the doctor's basement as splinters and bullets began to fly about. Then she went back to the ice-cream cornet business. I hope I shall see her again this summer.

*　　*　　*　　*　　*　　*　　*

The first big air battle that surprised us at 8.45 p.m. on Sunday 7 July was the beginning of a determined attempt to sweep our shipping off the sea and our aircraft from the skies. The *Luftwaffe* was feeling its way.

The diary for 8 July says " another big raid, scores of planes ", and again on the 10th, " big raid, planes and parachutes all over the sky. Several Germans brought down ".

This effort on 10 July was the most furious battle we had seen at that time over the Channel, and it began a period of violent and continuous air fighting which was to culminate in the massed " Battle of Britain " fights.

At least a hundred German bombers and fighters came

over on this afternoon to attack a convoy of ships at sea, and hundreds of bombs were loosed. They fell in clusters, and sent up great columns of water all round the vessels. In a matter of minutes Spitfires were taking up a counter attack on the enemy bombers. Machine-gun fire seemed to come from every part of the sky. Three of the raiders were shot down in as many minutes, and before the battle ended four more were sent diving vertically into the sea. It was a spectacle that left us gasping, and when it was over it was very difficult to put the story of these frenzied minutes into words.

On this occasion the raiders came over in two waves. I remember the stab that ran through me, like an electric shock, when I saw another forty bombers flying along towards the convoy, rather like a flock of wild duck. Fighters were buzzing over them like flies. Again bomb salvoes produced a solid wall of water in the air, which quite hid the little ships, and again Spitfires and Hurricanes turned to this new enemy formation, having already dealt with the first. In this action four more raiders were shot down and the rest were dispersed. At one time it was possible to count ten separate dog-fights in different parts of the sky. One of the raiders destroyed had its tail shot clean away and fell like a stone. Bombers and fighters alike were involved in this battle, and at one time there were some seventy machines engaged. Some were in combat, some were looking for opponents and the rest of the bombers were trying to find the best way out of the menace of circling Spitfires. It was an amazing spectacle, with the planes circling and darting in and out, manœuvring for position to get in bursts of fire. As planes fell in the sea it was not possible to say whether they were enemy or British. Some of the battles took place at the then popular height of ten thousand feet. Others were running fights just over the wave tops as Spitfires tried to fight their way past the escort of *Messerschmitts* on to the tail of the bombers. Some of the battles were two or three thousand feet above our heads on the cliff top. There was so much firing that we took cover eventually under ledges on the cliff.

I watched this, my first big massed battle, with almost unseeing eyes. There was too much to observe ; so much confusion, so much machine-gun fire in all directions that it was almost impossible to keep check on the movement. A boxing match is difficult enough to follow, but to see the real strategy of fights between scores of aircraft moving at anything from four to six miles a minute is almost impossible. Apart from the difficulty of understanding the tactics, there is the natural impulse just to look and watch, and to try to see everything. One turns from the start of one battle at the sound of another. Later experience showed that the only way to report an air battle is to follow one movement closely and let the rest look after itself.

During all this fighting the convoy of little ships, with fire spitting from their light guns and from the guns of their protecting destroyers, continued serenely down the Channel.

Some Folkestone fishermen who had been out in the thick of the battle, later came ashore and told their story. " Our fighters," one man said, " never gave the Germans a chance to get into accurate bombing position. One Nazi plane which had been shot down seemed like it was going to crash on our decks, but it flattened out and fell into the sea some way off. Two of the crew jumped out with parachutes but they did not open in time."

This was just one of a series of battles that for the next few months sprang up over and off Dover nearly every day.

They turned life into one long round of excitement from

AIR BATTLE OVER THE CHANNEL
Copyright: "Daily Mail."

morning until night. " Never a dull moment," was the catch-phrase among correspondents and photographers who found themselves involved in something new in modern warfare.

Everyone by now had a ' tin hat ' and would not think of going as far as the Post Office without it. Showers of ' shrapnel ' and bullets were liable to come down at shorter notice than a shower of rain. You could not buy a steel helmet in Dover in those days. They had to be obtained from London or elsewhere. I remember a colleague asking a military outfitter if he had a ' battle bowler '. " I'm afraid not," was the answer, " but I have a very nice line in hard hunting bowlers."

Dover people learned to move very quickly when these sudden air attacks developed, because most of them took place only a mile or so from the shore, and we had the backwash as they veered over the town.

Occasional night raids were also made on the harbour. One midnight there was a good deal of noise, and on hurrying the few yards to the promenade anti-aircraft shells could be seen bursting round a single raider. Suddenly there came a noise like the Flying Scotsman passing through a tunnel.

My colleague and I decided, with remarkable mental agility, that not only must this be a bomb, but that it was not very far away, as bombs fall. I sought protection behind an automatic chocolate machine, for the lesson of falling flat when in the vicinity of high explosives had not yet been learned. I am glad to relate that the bomb fell in the sea a hundred yards or so away. The chocolate machine swayed on its base, and I decided there and then that a personal interest in bombs was to be avoided whenever possible.

5

BOMBER ATTACK AND SMOKE SCREEN
Copyright: "Daily Mail."

Attacks of this nature continued nearly every day, until what came to be known at Dover as Black Thursday, 25 July, when five vessels in a convoy were sunk and five others damaged. But this was the Nazis' last real success in the Straits. It had been preceded by many other attacks. At any moment, during breakfast, lunch or dinner, we had been ready to leave the hotel and make for the promenade or Shakespeare Cliff, according to the apparent direction of the attack.

Here is a typical diary entry for that period :

Sunday 3.45 p.m. 14 July. Bombers attack convoys just outside harbour. Three ships damaged. Destroyer not hit but damaged. Five seamen killed on merchant ships. One of our fighters came down—pilot baled out. Seven Germans down.

Later that day a ship was brought into harbour with its stern blown off. About 40 *Junkers* 87 dive-bombers, as well as a number of ME 109 fighters, were engaged by the R.A.F. and anti-aircraft batteries. It was the period when the enemy was approaching his greatest effort.

For the next fortnight we lived in a state of constant alarm. Any whisper of a convoy approaching up the Straits sent photographers and correspondents scuttling up to the cliff top. It was a grim business, this peeping at death from a safe distance. It seemed almost more indecent than looking at an air battle. We would watch the approach of a convoy with the knowledge that any second the fatal first spout of water would be seen near one of the ships, to be followed by a bedlam of bombing and anti-aircraft fire as the attack developed. But at least we realised how much the Mercantile Marine was doing, and at that time there were millions of people in England who did not. I believe now that the graphic photographs and news reels produced by the men waiting on the cliffs played their part in showing people in safer areas that war was at last touching their coast.

On 19 July Mr. Gordon Selfridge came down, for apparently no other reason than to see some of the convoy battles. A generation ago he had acquired from Lord Northcliffe that frail box and string contraption with which Blériot, the French air pioneer, first crossed the Channel. Now the best aircraft that the world had seen were being used to bring death in its worst form. As we walked along the cliff the old man picked a wild flower and remarked on the beauty, simplicity and detail of each petal. I'm afraid it did not mean much to me, but I know that somewhere at the back of Selfridge's mind was a line of thought leading from the Blériot contraption to the *Junkers* 87. The statue of Blériot, once on Dover's sea-front, has been removed for safety. Perhaps it is just as well, for Blériot's peace of mind.

Their spirit could not be broken, yet our merchant seamen did not like being bombed and bombed and bombed again. I have seen some survivors, sometimes quite young boys, come ashore trembling from their experience. Sometimes the effect on them was similar to that on men who were continuously bombed at Dunkirk. On hearing an air-raid Alert they would look round for the nearest shelter, but they quickly recovered their nerve, and the bravest part of their trips was returning to sea again and again. It was quite common to meet men who had been mined or torpedoed three times. They would sit about the steps of the Seamen's Hostel, in strange clothes, waiting for travel arrangements to take them to their home port and another voyage of peril, but after an hour or so they recovered their nerve.

I remember in particular one South Wales crew who were brought ashore after having had to abandon their vessel—it was not sunk.

" And you can tell 'em," said one of these men defiantly, " they never will get us."

He was playing a game of darts in " Sailor Pub " as he told me the story—of how for an hour their skipper had manœuvred the vessel and defied the combined efforts of aircraft and " E " boats to sink them. They had been bombed from the air, machine-gunned and torpedoed by the " E " boats. The merchantman replied with Lewis and Tommy-gun fire and rifles. Two of the three torpedoes fired were cleverly avoided by the helmsman, but the third struck the bows. All the time the " E " boats were circling round her, sweeping the decks with machine-gun fire. This occurred before dawn, some miles at sea off Dungeness. When British aircraft appeared the enemy made off.

It was during this period that one of our destroyers, H.M.S. " Brazen ", was bombed and so badly damaged that she sank while being towed to port. But in the last moments of the attack her guns, blazing at point-blank range, took revenge. They brought down three of the Nazi planes. In the words of the Admiralty communiqué :

" One crashed alongside, the second received a direct hit in the nose with a three-inch shell, while the third received a direct hit abaft the port engine."

This bald narrative did less than justice.

One gunner had a wound above the eye, another in the leg, but he stuck to his gun and went on firing. All refused to leave their posts while there was still a chance of firing another shot.

The crew of the sinking destroyer cheered as they saw the attacking planes crash in the sea—cheered though they knew at any moment their ship might go down. Every member of the crew was saved. Some of the gunners had already taken toll of Hitler's navy in the Norwegian fighting.

This is a very inadequate account of a very brave action. If I had anything to do with propaganda good close-up photographs of those gunners, and their own story, would have been sent to the Press of every small nation, to South America and to the United States. The British Admiralty is notoriously conservative when it comes to a question of ' publicity '. Plenty of officers still do not like it. There has perhaps been some relenting lately, and men like A. J. McWhinnie, of my own paper, Ross White, the pawky Yorkshireman who photographs bursting shells and bombs for the *News Chronicle*, have done their part in bringing home to the people of the world what the Royal Navy and the Mercantile Marine are doing.

From the Mediterranean too have come very full accounts of the Navy's great victory over the Italian Fleet.

But it is not enough. There must be scores of stories hidden in the secluded modesty of wardrooms and messes, stories of heroism and gallantry, that would do their part no less than a twelve-inch shell in showing the world the kind of men we have. The submarine service must be brimming with deathless stories that have never been told and might well be, without any reference to operational movements.

At Dover I have found the naval authorities considerate. Commander " E. T." who has more than a full-time job in other directions, has been ready to help when he can. He paved the way for the splendid Dunkirk interview given by the Admiral, and for other services. We are still inclined to hear too little about the ordinary men of our forces, especially our patient, hard-working, but half-forgotten ' front line ' home army. I am sure wives and sisters would like to hear little personal intimate stories of how the men on the invasion front are waiting for the test.

* * * * * * *

25 July provided the longest day of sustained action Dover has known, and produced the biggest air battle

on record off the south-east coast, between 300 and 400 machines being engaged.

This was a day of continuous air fighting over Dover, followed by an action between our destroyers and German " E " boats off the French coast but in sight of our glasses. There were a hundred and one thrills packed into that day and photographers hardly knew which way to turn for dramatic incident. *Junkers* crashed into the sea, merchant ships were bombed and sunk before our eyes, destroyers survived what appeared to be a devastating dive-bombing attack and there were more dog-fights than the eye could follow.

Yet, while the full flood of war was on its very doorstep and ' ack-ack ' fire was loud and continuous, Dover carried on as usual.

We stood there on the cliff edge, breathlessly excited and futilely helpless. It seemed impossible that any of the little ships could survive the rain of bombs. Some did not. There were some twenty vessels of varying sizes in the convoy of that day when it was first attacked between Lydden Spout and Abbott's Cliff. Six of the merchantmen were sunk and two others damaged, but this loss was considerably less than the German claim of eleven ships totalling 43,000 tons.

Reading back now, I can see that the accounts of the battle at the time were hopelessly inadequate and did scant justice. There were so many emotions in the mind of the eye-witness. The first was for the crews of the ships. Sometimes their vessels were buried in spray but their Lewis guns fired all the time.

The dive-bombers came down in a follow-my-leader sweeping glide, until little more than mast-high. One saw the bombs leave the planes, but the effect of the explosions were lost in the walls of water thrown up. One thought of the men on board, with no deep shelters, their ships raked with splinters when not struck directly by a bomb.

As soon as the Nazi bombers had pounced out of the sky, shore batteries put up a protecting barrage and the R.A.F. fighters were soon busy, but the attack had been too sudden and the damage done before the *Junkers* could be driven off. One ship grounded off Shakespeare Cliff and photographers were amongst those who helped the crew ashore. I remember the skipper, himself injured, refused to leave until all his men had been taken off.

But the *Luftwaffe* itself suffered even heavier losses in fighters and dive-bombers in this attack. I saw several Nazis shot down in the sea, others were chased out of sight and destroyed off the French coast.

This was the Nazi dive-bombers' biggest, most determined and last big-scale shipping attack off the south-east coast. I doubt if it could be repeated to-day. But it is common knowledge that we had not then got the fighter strength, while the element of surprise was in favour of the enemy planes.

After the first phase of the attack the remaining vessels reassembled and steamed on. But their ordeal was not yet over. More waves of *Junkers* and *Messerschmitts* came out of the sky and the convoy was again attacked, this time between Abbot's Cliff and Folkestone, and one more ship was damaged.

By now the sky was thick with planes. The R.A.F. fighters had the situation under control, more black dive-bombers were shot down, the rest streaking for home. Then the enemy made a third attack, this time with " E " boats. They were determined the convoy should not escape.

As the remaining ships in convoy steamed out of sight I went down into Dover to meet the survivors of the damaged and sunk vessels. It was now about tea-time, and just as all seemed quiet, the last phase of the attack began. It was clear that the Nazis were making a desperate attempt to sink or damage all the ships. But this time their intention was foiled by our destroyers.

From my bedroom window, where I had gone to write the dive-bombing story, I saw two British destroyers streak out of the harbour and head straight towards the French coast, great wakes of white foam streaming from their sterns. A message had been received that " E " boats were following up the attack, and the destroyers were off to thwart it.

A fight followed between the destroyers and the German " E " boats—vessels similar to our motor torpedo boats, only rather larger. As the destroyers engaged the " E " boats in mid-channel they in turn were engaged by a further batch of enemy bombers. Flashes from the warships' guns could be seen directed at little black specks, which were the Nazi boats. From time to time the enemy tried to escape under cover of screens of white smoke. This sudden intervention was thrilling to watch, and it soon became clear that the " E " boats had been diverted from their objective. It was a miniature naval action and it was watched by many Dover people, from cliffs and promenade. Photographers crowded the roof of the hotel in the hope of securing long-range shots.

Then the destroyers' multiple pompom anti-aircraft guns went into action as a horde of *Stukas* dived from the clouds.

One by one they released their bombs and plumes of water could be seen leaping hundreds of feet into the air. Sometimes it seemed as if one of the destroyers had been struck, but she emerged again from a cloud of spume and smoke.

Chambermaids, the hotel manager, guests, all crowded at top-floor windows to watch the spectacle. There were many heart-beats when it seemed that one or both of the destroyers must suffer from the bombs that showered around them. But soon the noses of the destroyers were seen emerging from the spouts of water as they continued on their course. The sky buzzed like a hornets' nest with a host of Spitfires and Hurricanes diving to attack the Germans. No official claims were made at this time by the Admiralty because of the lack of certainty, but men who took part in the action believe they sunk or disabled four of the enemy " E " boats. And by now the convoy was miles away, streaming on in safety.

All this time there had been a series of violent dog-fights over Dover, as the course of the air battle swayed this way and that over the channel.

Finally the destroyers (it can now be said they were H.M. Ships " Boreas " and the " Brilliant ") returned to Dover. Both had been hit but not disabled. They were again bombed when on the point of reaching harbour, but for the last time our fighters met the *Stukas* and *Messerschmitts* and drove them off. There were some casualties in both warships, but they had done their part.

That was the end of one of Dover's most thrilling days.

The final Admiralty figures showed that during the action five vessels totalling 5014 tons were sunk and five others of 5133 tons received damage. But that day 28 Nazi planes were shot down for certain round the coasts of Britain, most of them as a result of the convoy attack.

While Dover itself suffered little or no damage, the town had been swept for hours by anti-aircraft and machine-gun fire. One running battle was carried on at roof-top height over the main streets. Two Spitfires, after an ME, hustled it at 300 miles an hour over the tops of houses, with the pursuers almost touching the tail of the Germans. Suddenly the ME dived low over the cliffs, the Spitfires followed, and a few more bursts sent the enemy machine hurtling into the water. There were many similar actions that day off Dover, and it is doubtful if any town has seen a bigger series of fights in such dramatic circumstances.

At such times, everyone in Dover was dodging ' shrapnel ' (or anti-aircraft shell fragments, as the purists would insist), and bullets from machine-gun fire.

I remember that, dashing back to the hotel, I passed a man on a ladder repairing a roof. As I walked by heavy firing broke out and he climbed down.

" It's a fair nuisance," he commented, " that's the sixth time this morning. Still, I'll get it done between the showers."

I must regretfully report that enemy action later made roof repairs at his particular premises unnecessary. At about the same time people sipping morning coffee in the main street were startled, if not disturbed, when machine-gun bullets cracked through the window. ' Shrapnel ' at this time was common in the streets. It would tinkle down at your feet or be lodged on the running-board of your car. I remember one man who said pleasantly he had found a bullet on his bed that morning.

During these attacks on shipping round Dover, correspondents and photographers were flocking into the town in search of what was then the first action of the war in this country. It became a commonplace to be drinking afternoon tea and eating thin sandwiches in the lounge of the Grand Hotel one moment, to be followed the next by a bedlam of every kind of anti-aircraft fire. When this burst out some wag would come out with the cry, " Tin-hat time, I think," or the comment, " Come to Dover. Visitors guaranteed never a dull moment."

There would be Guy Murchie, who wrote and photographed for the *Chicago Tribune*, out in his shirt sleeves, with movie camera on tripod, looking this way and that for an air battle to come within range, entirely unconcerned by the prospect of ' shrapnel '. In later days, after the

Grand was bombed, he dictated a first-class personal story before letting the hospital people treat him. This story, one of the best of the many produced from Dover, is reprinted later.

With Murchie would be half a dozen other photographers. Some would be perched perilously between the hotel chimney tops, an idea which was later stopped as the hotel people did not like the prospect of a dead photographer on their roof. Others lurked about the front.

The less brave of us, or the more cautious, dodged in and out of the doctor's doorstep. There was plenty to see and hear during these repeated and concentrated attacks on Dover harbour and shipping in the Straits.

On Saturday afternoon, 27 July, a British supply ship was hit and damaged in one attack, and later in the afternoon a destroyer was hit and sunk, with no casualties, by one of the luckiest or most skilful single bombs of the war. I saw the machine that obtained the hit come in from the sea, actually on the tail of a formation of our fighters. He dropped his lucky bomb and turned for home before anything could be done.

Sunday 28 July brought another big day of air battles, with practically continuous machine-gunning throughout the day. But as early as this, after a few weeks only, the air fighting was getting higher, and MEs and Spitfires began to look like flies. Once I looked out of the window just in time to see an ME driven down into the sea, some miles out, smoke pouring from its punctured fuselage. Soon after a torpedo boat raced out in the hope of picking up the pilot.

At the end of July, photographers lived with their cameras, took them to bed with them and to the bath. Several times I have known men leave their bath, expose a plate from the window on a fight or a machine bombing the harbour—and step back into the hot water!

On the Monday morning, 29 July, before breakfast, Dover Harbour had its biggest dive-bombing attack of all. I was just beginning to read the papers in bed, waiting for the morning tea, when the barrage began. It was no ordinary barrage, even for Dover, and explosions began to shake the room. My chambermaid popped her head in, excitedly. " I think you ought to see this," she said. By now there was a scurrying of people rushing upstairs and down, in dressing-gowns, with cameras. It was Dover's biggest and most spectacular attack of the war, and for the first time I for one began to feel nervous.

At least thirty *Junkers* dive-bombers and fifty *Messerschmitts* took part in this determined attack. It was for their work during this attack that later three men of the Dover Fire Brigade were awarded the George Medal. They were Sergeant Harmer, P. C. Brown, and Section Officer Campbell. They received the award for bravery on a blazing supply ship.

From the top-floor bathroom window the *Stukas* could be seen swooping down like huge black gulls, each dropping a bomb like a big black apple. It was a strange sensation to watch a big raid a few hundred yards distant and yet be comparatively safe—unless it happened that one of the *Stukas* happened to overshoot its mark.

A fairly good size oil fire was started as a result of this attack, but although dozens of bombs were bursting all over the harbour and around the ships in it, there was little damage.

For some time the *Stukas* came back again and again, going down mast high, swooping up and returning to the attack. In the meantime *Messerschmitts* tried to hold off our fighters as they sought to intercept the bombers. In the harbour everything was going off together—Lewis guns, Swedish Bofors guns (which made at least two direct hits that morning, blowing their victims to bits), light and heavy anti-aircraft guns and rifles. It is questionable which made the most noise, defences or bombs.

While this was on Dover people were scurrying to their nine o'clock work and the maid brought me my morning tea. And then suddenly all was silent. It was like that in Dover.

* * * * * * *

The worst bombing I ever saw was the cowardly attack on Folkestone Gate lightship, only about half a mile from the cliff where we stood with breathless anger and watched the *Stukas* come down.

It seemed to us a senseless attack, perhaps provoked by being frustrated from a more important target. Hilde Marchant, of the *Daily Express*, who has as fine a sense of the feel of the human side of things as anyone I know, was among us. She was furious and kept muttering " The rotten swine ", " The rotten swine " in sibilant tones under her breath. A couple of lorry-drivers had also pulled up and their views were rather stronger.

Two of the vessel's crew of nine were killed and others wounded.

I had been watching a dog-fight with some sixty machines engaged when I saw the six Nazi bombers, *Stukas*, swoop on the lightship. As each great black machine passed over at mast-height it dropped a large bomb. The first two fell in the sea on either side of the small craft, and we began to think it might escape destructon. Then the third seemed to be a direct hit, and we could not see exactly where the others fell for the wall of water that was flung up. The lightship was already sinking and a small dinghy pulled away from it with the injured survivors. There could be no possibility of the Nazi bombers mistaking the vessel for anything else than an unarmed lightship. German pilots had seen it for months swinging at its moorings and until then had not molested it.

In a matter of minutes the vessel began to settle and soon disappeared from sight. Four Spitfires saw to it that retribution quickly overtook the *Stukas*. They destroyed or damaged all of them. After their callous exploit the *Stukas* had streaked off towards France, but close behind them were the avenging Spitfires. We cheered as we saw the Spitfires overhaul the bombers and heard the opening bursts of machine-gun fire. Almost at once a *Stuka* wobbled, and it seemed to hop along the waves with a Spitfire a few feet above. There was more machine-gun fire and that *Stuka* blew up in a cloud of smoke and fragments. It was a most satisfactory destruction, and one of the rare cases in which we have felt no tinge of regret for the fate of the pilot.

Then the Spitfires chased the others, and it is believed two more were destroyed. The remaining three must have been hit and hard pressed to reach home.

The master of the lightship, Mr. James Eaton, was struck in the leg by a bullet, but when I saw him after he had left hospital he was anxious to get off to London and put in his report.

A week or two later we had an even more vivid close-up view of a dive-bombing attack, when the planes were so low and near that people on the cliff rushed for rifles. This time twenty-one dive-bombers, with a fighter escort above, swept in from across the Straits of Dover to attack a patrol of four small ships sailing a mile from the shore. Earlier in the day these ships, with others, had been shelled for hours without suffering damage.

I watched the aircraft coming in from the sea, wondering what their objective was. They seemed to be heading straight for the coast, almost as though coming inland. Then they dived to attack the ships which were so close inshore that they could not be seen until you were actually on the edge of the cliff. The Nazis dropped their bombs in turn and turned for home in a couple of minutes. Heavy anti-aircraft fire was bursting all round the machines as they came in for the attack when suddenly one went down in a steep dive to the sea. Some people thought it was hit, but it was in fact the typical almost vertical swoop of the dive-bomber. The pilot of this plane released a bomb and straightened out. Then the rest of the black machines with their tapering wings dived down in turn in a follow-my-leader formation. The bombs could be seen falling like apples, the ground shook from the explosions and great columns of water and smoke shot up. One of the ships caught fire and sank before it could reach harbour.

I have seen a lot of dive-bombing at close quarters and it is a terrible sight. One can picture the gunners. In small vessels they are exposed behind their Lewis or other light gun, finger on the button or trigger, summoning all their nerve to hold their fire until the last possible second. Men who have experienced this kind of thing tell me it is no good yielding to the natural temptation to blaze away as soon as the machines come into sight. To stand any reasonable chance of destroying them the gunner must wait until the last possible moment when the machine is turning into a dive and the bomb is about to be released. That takes a considerable amount of guts, but it is done. On the other hand dive-bombing is no joke for the pilot, who must have skill to judge the moment of his dive and straighten his machine up before his attack becomes his own death dive. Dive-bombing is one of the most devilish of all the horrible developments of air war. The dive-bomber however cannot hope for much success should there happen to be any fighters close to his target area. An element of surprise, diving unheralded from the clouds on to an unsuspecting target is the condition the dive-bomber likes.

*   *   *   *   *   *   *

It was too good to last, this living in the midst of war yet not being of it. And, as was inevitable, the Grand Hotel was later bombed one sunny afternoon. But during these exciting July weeks we were only witnessing the beginning of the 'Battle of Britain'. And it was still difficult to feel ourselves anything but spectators.

CHAPTER SIX

BALLOON-POTTING TO BATTLE OF BRITAIN

We did not realise it at the time, but this period of intensive attacks on shipping in the Channel was a preliminary to the great days of September, when the enemy put everything into an attack that failed.

The scale of the air war was gradually extending down the Channel to the Isle of Wight and beyond, but Dover remained the focal point of enemy action.

Looking back now it is possible to see some kind of picture of the German plan. The shipping attacks, which cannot be regarded as entirely unsuccessful, opened the way to other forms of attack. But at this period we only saw the *Luftwaffe* as a unit engaged in daily and apparently unrelated episodes. As newspaper men we were too engrossed with the immediate present to worry about the future.

8 August is described in notes made at the time :

" Biggest raid so far. German aircraft over Dover from 11 a.m. to 1.10 p.m. Terrific battles in the air. Two barrage balloons shot down. Extensive machine-gunning. Many planes in the sky. Five balloons in all shot down and some planes."

Some of the Nazis' most skilful and daring airmen came over regularly at this time on ' balloon-potting ' expeditions. If there have been any events in this war that could be regarded as having any element of sporting interest, it was these attempts to shoot down our balloons. After a month or two they ceased. The German losses were fairly regular, certainly out of all proportion to the material loss of balloons.

6

The first warning of these raids was usually the crack-crack-crack of the *Messerschmitt* machine guns as the plane dived suddenly out of the clouds, flew low over a balloon and tried to ' pot it '.

People in the streets learned to dive for the safety of doorways when this started, because bullets were flying around and in a minute or two our own ground defences were also in action, making the open streets decidedly unhealthy. The German pilots took great risks at this game, which was spectacular in the extreme. Sometimes the MEs would be met by our fighters, but usually each attempt would only last some ten minutes. During these scraps ' shrapnel ' was falling like rain, so much so that later troops were collecting it in buckets, to be used again against Jerry—at least that was the idea. I believe that technically it was never a very practical scheme.

It was common at this time to leap out of bed at 7.30 a.m. in time to see an ME roar by the window, machine guns firing at full blast. Sometimes the pilot would sweep out over the harbour, turn and come back for a second burst. But, usually, if the first shots failed the enemy would streak for home. They had to come down fairly low and within a few seconds of being seen would be facing a terrific barrage.

This was the time that the Dover area became christened ' Hell's Corner '. It was a German pilot who first used that phrase to describe the terrific barrage that was put up. Later, as the war on the Dover front developed, ' Hell's Corner ' became freely used as a synonym for a part of south-east Kent that experienced war months before the blitz was extended to the big cities and ports. But it was usually ' Hell's Corner ' for the attacker, not the defender.

Sometimes smoke would be seen coming from a balloon, which would gradually collapse, sag and fall, a blazing mass. Often five or six balloons would be brought down in this manner in a matter of a few minutes—and one or two *Messerschmitts*. As the destruction of a balloon could be written off as a cash loss of some £500, together with a certain loss of temper on the part of the perspiring ground staff, against a *Messerschmitt* at some £5000, not to mention the highly and expensively trained pilot, it will be seen that this Nazi sport was not really a paying proposition.

I have seen one of the balloon barrage service lorries trundling round the town with the motto chalked on the side ' You knock 'em down—we put 'em up '.

One morning five balloons were shot down between 7.30 a.m. and 8.15 a.m., followed by a couple more at noon. This cost the enemy two *Messerschmitts* and the people really annoyed were the men who had to run up new balloons. You could see them struggling with thousands of feet of cable lying in a tangled mass on streets and roof tops, and making numerous uncomplimentary remarks on the Nazi airmen.

In the end the balloon men played their own part in defending their balloons. I have seen squads of them on roof tops blazing away with rifles at the black Nazi machines as they swooped and dived among the balloons. One morning they claimed the destruction of an ME, but as similar claims were made by at least four other gun crews the matter was never really settled. However, the balloon men remained happy in their own minds that they had destroyed the raider, and it cheered them up a lot to think of it next time one of their toys came down in flames.

The biggest balloon strafe on record came one fine Saturday morning at the end of August, and no one knows to this day what was the real motive behind it.

We were having breakfast when the usual blitz started outside the windows. As it was Saturday, and our day off, the correspondents did not take much notice until we began to realise that balloons were coming down much faster than usual, and there were at least a dozen Nazi machines engaged in the attack. That morning some twenty balloons were shot down within an hour, and as they went about their week-end shopping Dover people began to wonder what was going to happen next. Most people thought that this complete and determined destruction indicated a new large-scale attack on the harbour.

The balloon barrage people were frantic, but an hour or so after the last one had been shot down in flames the first of a new lot of balloons slowly ascended, to our great relief. It was followed by another here and another there, and long before lunch our full protective barrage was again floating over the town. It was a grand high-speed effort, but the enemy had not finished. They came back in the evening and shot down thirteen more, which were as promptly replaced by new ones.

It was the balloon-potters' most successful day, but it cost them at least four machines, so they were still well out on the debit side.

Most of the pilots on this game seemed crack men—at times their daring won admiration even from the men who had to run out and struggle with the twisted wire and burned fabric before a new balloon could be run up.

One vivid impression, typical of this period, remains in my mind. An attacking *Messerschmitt*, sweeping out of the sun at some 400 miles an hour, set fire to a balloon and raced away. White shell puffs appeared near its tail. It rocked and crashed into the sea. The pilot baled out.

Our fighters, too, adopted new tactics which resulted in a number of the enemy being destroyed. As the MEs played among the balloons, high-flying Spitfires shot out to sea and ambushed the enemy as they turned for home.

These episodes of the balloons were comparatively small

interludes in the interval between the convoy attacks and the massed daylight raids on the country.

Various reasons have been suggested to account for these raids. They never seemed to have much operational value, except on that Saturday when the attack was never followed up. One suggestion was that the raids formed part of the pilots' training, perhaps as a preliminary to shooting down the bigger barrages round London and other cities. Whatever the motive, balloon-potting proved to be an expensive and impractical proposition. Once or twice violent electrical storms produced the same effect, balloons catching fire and floating helplessly to the ground as lightning struck among them.

*   *   *   *   *   *   *

This was the period when the enemy was launching his early daylight formations against England—and already paying far too heavily for the attempt.

Between 11 and 18 August between 600 and 700 enemy machines were destroyed in raids on this country, and much of the fighting and interception took place in the Dover area and the belt of country extending back to Canterbury, Ashford and Maidstone.

Day after day we watched planes crash in flames on sea and land, saw pilots bale out, heard the thud of bombs and the crash of anti-aircraft fire. Some days, all day, day after day, there was a constant heavy drone in the air as formation after formation of *Dorniers* passed over to London and other inland objectives.

Five hundred aeroplanes might cross the Channel in a few hours. Ding-dong battles would take place high over the sea along miles of coastline. Life was hectic.

I have seen as many as seven machines come down in the space of an hour. Dover itself was not being heavily bombed now. But there was always the risk from bombs dropped by harassed enemy machines.

By the beginning of August American correspondents had arrived by the dozen and here, for the first time, they were seeing real action. Helen Kirkpatrick, of the *Chicago Daily News*, Virginia Cowles of the *New York Herald-Tribune*, Vincent Sheean, Ben Robertson of the New York *P.M.*, and Bob Casey, with dozens of others, here found material to satisfy the most dramatic pen.

We all knew we were outnumbered in the air. But it did not seem to affect the issue once a few of our fighter pilots got into the air.

One of the most dramatic of my personal experiences of the men who saved the country occurred a few miles from Dover.

Overhead I saw a great swarm of German bombers and fighters heading inland, making for London. They had passed safely through a heavy barrage and were going on. They were passing over when machine-gun fire broke out. And I gasped, because I realised that there, among those hundred and fifty or more *Dorniers* and *Messerschmitts*, was a Spitfire. Actually, it became known later, six or seven of our fighters had taken on that cloud, turned and dispersed the Nazis and brought down at least four. It was a magnificent effort.

The first German machine fell almost at my feet. There suddenly came from the sky that high-pitched scream, continuing to a roar, which means that a mass of metal is hurtling down out of control at some four or five hundred miles an hour. The crash came a couple of fields away. The wreckage, in thousands of pieces, was spread over three fields. It was marked by a myriad wisps of smoke. Some of the pilot's maps were strewn over the field. They showed he had been over Poland and France before finding these less healthy British skies. A handful of country people watched this action and they talked about it later with awe, admiration and thanks. I have the enemy pilot's chased leather belt as a souvenir. Not far away I watched the pilot of another ' winged ' *Messerschmitt* bale out and land not far away. That formation never reached its objective.

We on the spot still did not realise the significance of the battles we were watching. We were too close to see the drama in perspective. But these days marked the beginning of our big air successes. I remember one lunch-time, an officer came in and said, " Well, it's sixty so far, they can't keep that up ", and, as during Dunkirk, it began to be realised we were in the middle of a bigger battle than we knew.

I say ' we ', but it was those immortal ' few ' who were doing the work.

The story of these days is beginning to be told in official and other publications. But at Dover, even if we did not grasp the whole story, we saw more of the actual fighting than people in any other part of the country.

During this phase thousands of bombs were dropped over the countryside around us. No one knows how many, but the scattered enemy forces dropped them like rain.

At first we began to rush out to the scene of crashed enemy planes. Later this became an impossibility—there were too many, and the carcass of one *Dornier* looks very like that of another.

Every day newly arrived British and German airmen alike were being treated in Dover hospitals. Most of the Germans were truculent and suspicious. They would not have an anæsthetic, they would not have this and that. They would not co-operate. One Nazi refused a cup of tea because he thought it might be poisoned. But the doctors went on with their job, regardless of protests. Often, after a few days, the Nazis became comparatively human. A British sergeant pilot met in a ward a German pilot who had been engaged in the same battle. They glared at each other for a few minutes and then got talking.

Another German pilot made a forced landing on a certain aerodrome. The guards rushed up to him and as he stepped from the machine he asked where he was. " You are at so-and-so," he was told, being given the name of the aerodrome. " Oh no," grinned the Nazi, with a you-can't-diddle-me air, " oh no, so-and-so finish . . . poof," indicating that his bomber friends had written that particular aerodrome off. He was quite surprised to learn that the aerodrome was far from written off, as his friends had no doubt led the Fatherland authorities to believe. Actually a good many buildings at this aerodrome were demolished or damaged, but the aerodrome was nearly always in use. Bomb craters were filled in almost as soon as made.

At this time we also heard a number of circumstantial stories of German airmen, when captured, asking the whereabouts of the nearest German troops. I was not able to obtain such a story at first-hand but I am satisfied they are true. There is no doubt that the Nazis themselves were hopelessly deceived about the success of their attacks. Each successive wave of Nazi airmen who came over thought they were on to a good thing. I can imagine some interesting scenes when it later came to comparing notes in prison camps.

It became known at this time that enemy raiding squadrons, or what was left of them, returned to other than their own home stations, because it was necessary to keep the true facts of the losses caused during raids over Britain from spreading among the personnel of the *Luftwaffe*.

* * * * * * *

Still, as the August days went by, the mass formations kept coming over. They no doubt believed that constant battering would wear our fighter strength down until it became a negligible force.

Dover's Alerts had reached the 100 mark. Sometimes there were as many as ten in a day.

Mr. Winston Churchill came down on one of Dover's biggest days and saw for himself how the Germans were being shot from the sky. During his tour of the area and from the casemates of Dover Castle he saw seven enemy machines destroyed.

This diary entry is typical of those crowded days :

" *Saturday 24 August 1940.*—Siren at 8 a.m. and four warnings covered the whole morning. Plane in sea. Saw 25 bombers go inland. Much fighting in the air and plenty of a.a. fire. Siren again 1.10 p.m. Saw 3 planes down, 2 baling out. Jerry came back from inland and burst two balloons on way out. Terrific barrage put up. Dover area shelled from Cap Griz Nez between 5 and 6 p.m. No damage to property or persons. Fell in fields. Bomber crashed in Elms Vale killing Police-constable Maycock and his wife. Crew of 5 also killed."

This is a pretty fair summary of the daily alarms and excursions of this period. Often one did not know which way to turn to keep pace with events. As soon as one set off on one inquiry something else would start. It was an American correspondent who coined the phrase " ten-dollar box " when describing the anti-aircraft fire.

" It used to be a five-dollar box of fireworks," said the Yankee reporter. " Now you are bringing out the ten-dollar box."

It was another American correspondent who made history at the time (you must remember that this was before London's blitz days and nights) by describing his bombing experiences while waiting to be operated on in hospital.

It was the day the Grand Hotel was bombed, as well as a number of other buildings in the area, including the little " Sailor Pub " where I had seen so much of the war spirit of Dover's people.

This day, 11 September, was, as I shall describe later, one of the most important in the war, and one when invasion was more imminent, in my opinion, than any time before or since. I had arranged to be out of the hotel the afternoon of the bombing, as were most people.

The *Chicago Tribune* headline was :

WRITER INJURED IN AIR RAID 'PHONED THIS TALE OF HORROR. ESCAPED FROM DÉBRIS OF HOTEL AND STAYED ON JOB AS HE AWAITED OPERATION.

London, *11 September.*

Shortly after undergoing a terrifying experience which might have unnerved the bravest of men, Guy Murchie, lying in a hospital bed in pain and waiting for a doctor to cauterise and stitch his wounds, to-night telephoned from Dover as calmly as if nothing unusual was happening.

This was his story :

" A hotel in the Dover area frequented by newspaper men was hit by an aerial bomb to-day and one whole end of it fell in ruins.

" This correspondent, now threatened with a general anæsthetic in hospital, happened to be in the wrong end of the top floor at the crucial moment and fell four storeys with collapsing débris.

" Here is the direct story of how it felt to be the victim of a direct hit by Fuehrer Adolf Hitler's air force. Stanley (Massa) Johnstone, of the *Chicago Tribune's* London staff, and I were talking with two naval officers in a room on the west end of the hotel's top floor. An air-raid warning was on and anti-aircraft fire was potting white spots against the sunset. I happened to lean out of the window and saw twelve Nazi bombers directly overhead. I remarked to my three friends, ' Twelve of them are exactly above now. If they have dropped anything, it will hit in about 15 seconds.'"

(Fifteen seconds is too generous an allowance. It is about four.—R. F.)

" Then we heard a swishing sound, followed by a terrific explosion. The bomb obviously landed in the street outside.

" Two seconds later the loudest bang I have ever heard went off directly overhead. I afterwards learned it must have been within ten or fifteen feet of my head on the roof above. I held my arms over my head instinctively. Everything went black. I was fully conscious as the floor fell away under my feet. I remember congratulating myself on my luck in being uninjured. As I dropped into emptiness the air was black, full of soot. I expected to land on the next floor, but to my surprise, I kept falling for many seconds. I waited, limply, feeling that this might be the end for me . . . then I landed. It did not hurt but everything was pitch black. There were sounds of crumbling wreckage. I held my arms over my head again and moved my hands over a beam that I could feel just above me. The bombs were still exploding and anti-aircraft fire resounded. A few shouts and cries could be heard from the débris.

" Gradually the air grew lighter as the smoke and soot settled, and I could see I was tangled in a mass of timbers. The remaining jagged walls towered upward some fifty feet and I was acutely aware of the possibility of one of them falling on me.

" I climbed out of the débris, elated to be alive. Then I saw Johnstone climb out near me, his face back with soot. We shook hands.

" I heard a girl calling ' Please help me. Please get this beam off me.' · She was about twenty feet away. Her face was black, but I recognised her as the pretty hotel receptionist. I tried to haul away the timber.

" Johnstone, apparently uninjured, went away for help. The girl was in great pain, but suppressing her agony. Her leg appeared to have been broken and as I pulled away débris I could see she was bleeding badly. Unable to move the timber I climbed down to the street and found a soldier who got me a saw with which I soon was able to saw the timber and free the girl.

" About this time I realised I was limping and had some bad cuts on my legs. After recovering some luggage from my room in the undamaged part of the hotel I was taken to hospital. The injured girl is now in the next bed to my own, after having been given a pain-killing drug and being prepared for an operation. I have just heard that one of the naval officers with me in the hotel survived with a few cuts on the head. The other is feared dead. Bombs and guns are still booming as I write.

" I must now phone this story to London because my relatively slight operation comes next."

That is probably one of the best personal accounts of an air raid yet written.

And what did Dover itself do during those great, those dramatic days when one of the world's greatest battles was fought in its skies ?

The only concession shopkeepers made when a raid was in progress was to put up their shutters—the majority of them have only got wooden shutters anyway at the moment. Many of the assistants and customers hurried off, with tin hat and gas mask, to A.R.P. or fire posts.

Council meetings continued as usual, raids or no raids. The fact of an air-raid warning was flashed on cinema screens or announced by the manager of the Hippodrome, but, as elsewhere, few took any notice. I have seen Service men and civilians suddenly drop flat on the floor of a bar when a bomb has fallen near and continue a second or two later talking and drinking.

*   *   *   *   *   *   *

I do not want to write much about Dover's bombs. Too many people since have had too many terrible experiences, and that form of death and destruction is not nice to write about and not very pleasant reading.

There is no reason to suppose that the spirit of the people of London, Swansea, the Clyde, Bristol, Coventry and the rest is any inferior to that of the people of Dover, and their sufferings have been worse. But I think Dover helped set the example of how to carry on. It was the first town to react to bombing and shelling. The reaction was the same that has been noticed all over the country. A little Union Jack would appear in the midst of a heap of rubble. Shopkeepers launched those little destruction-defying phrases that have become a part of our national life. " Not much in the windows but plenty inside "—" Business as usual—we hope ". The Hippodrome issued its " To hell with Hitler and his unexploded bombs " poster which gave an alternative approach to the theatre when the main road running by it was closed because of an unexploded bomb. The barber who used to shave me while gunfire was on outside remarked soothingly, " It's all right, my hand won't slip ". Occasionally, on noisy nights, the bar of the Grand Hotel would close because of a glass roof overhead. The bar would be temporarily transferred to the reception office. We used to call it the Dispensary or First Aid Station.

Towards the end of August, Dover had some slight distinction in the bombing news. It received the first and probably only Italian bombs to fall in this country. One afternoon in the late autumn we saw something new in a formation of bombers and fighters. There were some nine large bombers and the usual swarm of fighters, appearing to be flying quite low.

" What on earth are they ? " we asked. They did not seem to correspond with our quite extensive knowledge of *Dorniers*, *Junkers* and the rest. Nothing on the charts seemed to fit the design.

Tom Moore, our landlord at the " Royal Oak ", high up, almost on the edge of the cliff, which became our headquarters when the Grand was bombed, turned his telescope on the strange fleet. We had begun to think in terms of troop-carrying planes and things like that.

Then he saw their exotic pale green and light blue colouring and the two black markings known now as the Italian call-sign, which looked at that time rather like a capital H.

"They're Wops," he said, and it was later confirmed that the bombers were *Savoia* 79's, and among the fighters were a large number of CR 42's—Italian fighter biplanes.

They soon began to drop their bombs. We could see them leave the machines. But the bombing attempt was not more successful than the Italian planes proved on that and the second occasion they made a trip to these coasts. One bomb did comparatively slight damage in the town. A number fell in the harbour : others fell in the town and did not explode until later. A large number fell in open country. It looked as though the bombs were more or less shovelled overboard.

The Italian planes did not stay very long. The big machines made good targets for the anti-aircraft people, who straddled them with accurate bursts. After a short tour a few miles inland, parallel with the coast, they turned and made for home.

Spitfires were soon in the air giving chase and followed them well over the French coast. I doubt if the Italians spent more than five minutes over the county of Kent.

There was considerable shyness on the part of the authorities at the time in admitting the presence of these Italian visitors. In those days we were, so to speak, still arguing on the precipice with Italy. There were half-hearted attempts next day by some papers to deny that there were ever any Italian planes over at all. There was certainly no mention of the bombs. It seemed at the time that we rather hoped that Italy " didn't really mean it ". (Things are different now.)

The Italians tried again a few weeks later and lost more than a dozen machines off the Thames Estuary. After that the Italian air force ceased to compete with the *Luftwaffe* for the honour of sharing the daylight raids over Britain.

The formation we saw would have been easy meat for two or three Hurricanes. Twenty-two raiders were brought down that day, including a good number of our Italian friends. But at this time the air fighting itself was changing. We were already passing from the ' Battle of Britain ' to the next, the ' Invasion ' phase.

CHAPTER SEVEN

WAITING FOR THE INVASION

As the summer of 1940 sped by in a blaze of glory for the Royal Air Force and a succession of turbulent days for the rest of us, the Battle of Britain developed into the invasion threat.

On the night of 11 September the Premier gave a broadcast warning that the long-threatened invasion attempt might be launched at any time.

On that day the Admiralty had issued a brief *communiqué* :

" *Strong and repeated offensive actions are being taken by our light naval forces against German shipping movements, ports and concentrations of shipping.*

" *These operations have inflicted losses upon the enemy, as well as damage to port facilities which would be vital to him in the event of an attempt to invade England.*

" *Further details cannot be given without disclosing information which would be useful to the enemy.*"

For my part I think indeed that this period from 7 September to about 15 September, when the number of enemy machines destroyed over this country reached the record figure of 185, was the most critical we have gone through.

It had been reported earlier in the month that the enemy were evacuating civilians from the Channel port areas. Saturday 7 September was the day of one of the biggest air raids on London. In the late afternoon raid, the Nazis succeeded in dropping a considerable number of bombs on the London dock area, but the attempt cost them over a hundred machines.

The next day, 8 September, the Royal Air Force was busy bombing the coast of France, and repeated these raids every night.

During this week of tension there were fluctuations in the amount of enemy air action. On some days we only had the opportunity of bringing down two or three machines.

At Dover, new American correspondents were arriving daily, and Shakespeare Cliff and hotel roof tops became a kind of grand stand. There were photographers, cinema men, the B.B.C. was represented, the Columbia Broadcasting Company of America was there. It was a strange, exciting atmosphere, yet unreal, because if there had been an invasion attempt I do not think it could have been reported sitting on the top of a cliff ! But no one seemed to worry about that.

9 September is described briefly in my diary as " big shelling day ", but there appears to have been only one air-raid warning.

It had been a strenuous time and I felt like sleep and a little letter-writing, but in the end we went up to the cliff in case something happened. It did.

We saw one of the most astonishing sights of the war, which quite explained the subsequent Admiralty *communiqué*. And, in addition, by going to the cliff, we escaped the bombing of our hotel an hour or so later.

We were sitting lazily in the sunshine, half-way down the cliff. The sky was blue, the sun hot, there was a buzzing of insects in the air, but not a sound of aircraft, and war seemed far distant. We even remarked to each other, dreamily, that there did not seem ' to be much doing ' and in a vague way wondered why.

Having almost written the day off as ' quiet ', we suddenly heard a great burst of air activity. Shrapnel began splashing in the sea below us like hailstones, some of it pattering down on rocks near by. It occurred to both

7

of us that it would be a sound idea to go up to the cliff-top café for a cup of tea. " Tin-hat time," said my friend, but it did not seem more than that.

From the porch of the tea-room we saw a flight of bombers heading towards Dover, with the usual fighter escort. Shelling also began—and it seemed that Dover was in for a bad time. Then we saw something more unusual to distract our attention even from bombing, shelling and air battles.

" Look at those ships—seven of 'em—what are they ? " someone said.

From the cliffs I looked out to sea, and with my glasses began to pick out the shapes of several biggish vessels. Then we went to the attic of the "Royal Oak" and trained Tom's large telescope on the scene. We picked out more ships, first eight, then nine, then ten. They were standing in close to the French coast and were moving in the direction of Calais from Boulogne.

While we were excitedly trying to pick out these vessels big air battles were raging over Dover. There was the sound of bombs exploding and a heavy anti-aircraft barrage. Shells were also falling in the Dover area. We remarked at the time that the bombs seemed to be falling on the town itself—we could see the smoke clouds—and turned, as it seemed to us, to the more important matter of the ships. There were one or two soldiers on the scene by now and a few civilians who, attracted by the noise, had stopped their cars. As we focused our eyes across the Channel and got accustomed to the light, more and more ships came into view, standing out in a long line as though in battle formation. We finally counted more than thirty grey ships in that convoy and I have since heard that the actual number was more than seventy. Taken in conjunction with the shelling and the air raid it seemed very significant. I remember rushing to the telephone with confused thoughts at the back of my mind that this might be an invasion move. It seemed that anything might happen in the next hours and that I might not be able to telephone at all. As we now know, nothing happened then or that night or on the anxious days that followed. The answer is in the hands of the Admiralty, the Royal Air Force and the German Command.

I remember telling the office that something unusual was afoot, and then we turned to watch the ships until they disappeared from sight in the haze and distance. They were of all sizes, some big cargo vessels, some small, but the majority large, and there appeared to be several warships among them. It was the first and only time I have seen any large gathering of enemy ships, although I have several times since seen them in small convoys of three and four.

Driving into Dover we found that considerable damage had been done in the town ; a seamen's hostel, a garage, a café, public houses and other buildings were destroyed or damaged. It was in one of these small public houses that Mr. Francis Richardson and his wife Grace, daughter Joan and mother, aged 69, were trapped and killed. There were a number of other deaths in the town, including Mr. and Mrs. W. E. Cook, stewards at the hostel. This was our first experience of considerable bombing, and we did not like it. Already squads of sweating troops were at work moving masses of débris. I remember the balloon barrage man who was found trapped. He was talking and said he was quite all right, but he died when they got him out. People everywhere have suffered this, and worse, since, but in those days it brought to us a terrible realisation of war. We tried to help in the rescue ; we were worried about our own colleagues, and at the back of our minds was the thought of what might happen next, or anyway that night.

Gradually order came out of the chaos. There were two deaths in the hotel, a naval officer who had been on the same floor from which the American correspondents escaped, and a kitchen hand who had been trapped in the basement. Just now I have seen a colleague of his who escaped and is still, after ten months, receiving hospital treatment.

Two photographers, Freddie Girling, of the *News Chronicle* and " Dixie " Dean, of the *Daily Mirror*, were blackened and grimed like sweeps, and they too worked hard to rescue some of the injured. We were more than relieved to find our close friend, Geoffrey Edwards of the *News Chronicle*, beaming through his glasses, while his colleague H. D. Harrison said that he congratulated himself on having been playing billiards at the time the bomb fell. In the basement he crawled under the table when the bombs began to fall, and felt quite safe. When he crawled out he found he had not been under the table at all, but he considered it a comforting thought at the time. An American correspondent pocketed the pink as a souvenir.

After the first shock we had no time to worry much about the bombing. It seemed there might be even bigger events afoot. I thought at the time that the bombing attack was a diversion to cover the convoy : it was hardly big enough or sustained enough for anything else. In fact we all believed the invasion threat at that time was very real.

I heard later that evening that the enemy convoy had put out a smoke screen to cover its movements. British bombers were seen flying towards the spot where the ships had last been seen and there was the sound of war all that night. There were continual flashes and explosions from the other side of the Channel. It was the beginning of a period of sustained air and sea attack that undoubtedly smashed concentrations of men, barges and other invasion material then gathered in the Channel ports.

This was the occasion when poor Councillor J. Walker, who in earlier days had told the Council just what he thought of the idea that he and others should run away, was killed by a shell fragment during the bombing. He was tending his motor boat on the beach. The petrol in the boat caught fire and the charred remains of his dog were found by his side. A newsboy, struck on the head with splinters, was taken to hospital still clutching his bundle of papers.

Vice-Admiral Sir Bertram Ramsay had a narrow escape from a flying splinter that afternoon. There was considerable damage in the town. Dozens of shop fronts were wrecked. One bomber crashed in the sea following a direct hit from anti-aircraft fire.

That night the R.A.F. attack on Hitler's invasion fleet was intensified. We saw the flashes and heard the thuds as the bombers swooped on his barge concentrations and shipping lurking in harbours and docks along the whole of the Channel coast.

For the next few days we looked across the Straits of Dover peering on Hitler's invasion moves, wondering what would happen next. It was a thrilling place to be in. Through glasses I could see barges in Calais harbour and military preparations along our coast stiffened every day.

Then there was a lull of a few days until 15 September, which is briefly recorded in my diary as " another big day : scores of dog-fights ". This was the day when the R.A.F. made their record bag of 185 machines, and only on one day since, later in the month, have they had the opportunity to again exceed the century. That day, I think, virtually marked the end of the critical period.

But on this day planes were all over the sky. The enemy was flinging his mass formations across, almost for the last time that year. A day or two later it began to be clear that the R.A.F. had broken the back of the *Luftwaffe*.

Five days later, on 20 September, another 200 Nazi planes crossed the coast, heading for London, but they were soon broken by our fighter formations and sent scuttling back.

There had been, however, a number of invasion scares and alarms during this late August–end-of-September period. Late one August night, in the Grand Hotel, when bugles began sounding up and down the coast from point to point along the cliffs, we thought that some big move was imminent. It was an exciting moment then, but, as I now understand, the alarm was based on mistaken information. Wiseacres said dramatically they had heard bugles many times, but " never bugling like that ". It was said that the bugles were sounding the ' general alarm '. I went out into the street and found wondering Dover citizens popping their heads out of windows. Some-one in the Home Guard said that this was the ' real thing ' and began issuing ammunition.

An excited soldier came in for a certain officer who was wanted ' very urgently '. One or two people began to pack their bags and cameras in case the Nazis came up the shingle a little later, and others stood in knots at the corner of the street, talking and speculating, as people do when something is afoot. I sat on the hotel stairs with a bunch of other correspondents and we telephoned vague accounts to our offices. It never occurred to us at the time that we would never have been able to do this had anything really vital been in the wind. After an hour or so a friendly policeman came in and said " It's all right now ", and I wouldn't swear, but I believe he may have had a drink. It was said next day that the cause of the commotion was a report sent from a patrol ship off the south coast, but that it had been based on a misconception, but the full truth was never told. We all went to bed quite happily after the exciting hour, and waited for the next day's round of air battles.

It is now known that a combination of circumstances was responsible for a general alarm, from Whitehall right down to the coast defences. Apart from the patrol ship's report an enemy convoy had been sighted. Taken together there seemed every justification for circulating the codeword which was at that time being used to give warning of imminent invasion danger. It can be said now the codeword then was the name of one of this country's greatest military and political figures.

Even now it still seems certain that no invasion attempt was ever actually launched during those momentous days. It was so near, yet still so far.

On Sunday 22 September there was another 'flap' as we came to call these recurring invasion scares. At various military centres the general alarm was again sounded at 3 p.m. and 9 p.m., and troops were recalled from cinemas and amusements. Again I have no reason to suppose this was based on anything of a serious nature.

Various suggestions have been made from American sources that Hitler did actually start his invasion during this September period, and that many thousands of troops were caught and destroyed 'in burning water' as they were about to set off in their barges. My own impression is that the word 'off' was never given. That we were very near to being invaded in these autumn days is certain, but I think between 7 and 15 September and thereabouts the Navy and R.A.F. showered such a rain of destruction along what is now called the Invasion Coast that it was never possible for the move to be launched. I have no doubt that the enemy lost thousands of troops who were then concentrated in that area, but my view is that they were lost, not in making the attempt, but before they could make it.   It is possible that some were attacked and destroyed during embarkation exercises, but I do not think the ' invasion attempt ' went far beyond that.

A number of bodies of German troops were washed up at various points along the south-east coast, but I have been unable to confirm some reports that they were in any considerable quantities.   There has also been found a certain amount of wreckage of possible invasion barges.

No, I think Hitler just could not do it then.

But if the invasion threat was quelled then, it has not been entirely removed.   At Dover the state of tension lasted periodically all through the winter.   At that time I and my colleagues had visions of going home for a week or two, but there was always sufficient incident to make it seem unwise. Possibly this reaction was all part of the ' war of nerves ', but it seemed more than likely that Hitler would use the winter months to refit and replan his campaigns.

For a long time there was action nearly every day, shelling, desultory bombing and air fighting, but never on the same lavish scale as during those summer months when, I am convinced, the Nazi High Command had put everything they knew into an attack that failed.   By October the big days had gone, and it was only on odd days that the R.A.F. bag reached double figures.

But the enemy-occupied Channel ports were given no peace.   It seemed that part of our aim was to make the country round the northern coast of France gradually untenable for military purposes.   Very often, at night, the same sinister roll is heard across the Channel as during those more threatening days.

On 30 September we watched for hours war on both sides of the Channel.   We were shelled, enemy ships bombed and shelled.   If the shadow of invasion had grown thinner, it was still there.

That night the French coast was illuminated as the

R.A.F. hammered again at what remained of the enemy's invasion concentrations. That was the day we bombed and shelled another big enemy convoy. It was clear that if invasion had been made to lie down it was not dead.

By this time the Germans were gradually increasing the number of their big gun emplacements, but it began to appear that a strongly armed coastline such as they were building up would be as valuable for defence as for attacks. It is known the enemy now has a considerable number of coastal guns of all calibres.

The Christmas period produced a ' flap ', but I doubt if the extra precautions taken were much more than a safeguard. There was perfect ' invasion ' weather in the Straits for several days—a calm sea and a blanket of mist. On Monday 23 December the R.A.F. had made another big attack on the coastal ports and for the next few days there seemed the possibility that the enemy would attempt, if not a full-scale invasion, at least some diversion. Our coastal defences were and are always prepared to meet small sudden snap landing parties, sent over by the enemy partly in the hope of picking up information and partly in the hope of securing prisoners. It was thought that the winter nights would be taken advantage of to send over such raiding parties, but I have not heard of any appearing.

On Saturday 28 December the most bombed piece of coastline in Europe, between Calais and Boulogne, had its heaviest attack for months. Although they had seen dozens of similar attacks, bus conductors on the coastal routes, farm workers and people living in cliff-top houses all commented on the violence of the attack.

Certainly all during that Christmas week the R.A.F. gave plenty of attention to the ' Invasion Coast '. But I do not think there was much more to be read into that activity than the R.A.F.'s known policy of preventing the enemy from settling down to any plan of concentration.

It is a matter of policy for every new report of troop concentrations, assembling of equipment or of new gun emplacements to be followed by yet another coastal raid. It is obviously going to make any new invasion plans from that part of the coast difficult to carry out if they are met with heavy and sustained bombing as soon as sighted. This is a matter of common sense, but I leave it to the reader to put his own interpretation on the fact.

So Dover enjoyed a peaceful Christmas. Three cinemas and a music hall were open on Christmas day and there was a public dance until midnight.

By December of 1940 Dover had come through the most pulsating year in its long history.

* * * * * * *

Most people in Dover believe that should an invasion ever be launched the " Gateway to England " must necessarily be well in the battle ground. Its geographical position seems to make that certain.

It is reasonable to suppose that any invasion scheme would have to include several surprises on the part of the enemy, as Hitler well realises our precautions are many and complete. He might try and counter these with some new technique which it might be supposed our Service experts have not thought of. All I can say is that any surprises produced would not be all on one side. But at this stage of the war, with Act 2 hardly opened and the final curtain not in sight, invasion theories are worse than useless. I have heard scores of arguments of every kind, dozens of theories and suggestions as to how this, that and the other might be attempted. It is a waste of time to record these hypothetical ideas. Besides, I might inadvertently put ideas into the wickedest brain in Europe. Intelligence people may have good ideas, when and if the time comes, about the distribution and possible intended use of German military concentrations.

Activity overhead or not, Dover remains the most interesting town in England, and ' if it starts all over again ' everybody—from the Admiral, the Brigadier, the Mayor and the Chief Constable to the oyster man and the billiard marker—will be ready to meet it.

Dominating Dover is the Castle, with its long line of Constables through history, from King Harold II in 1053 to the famous Hubert de Burgh in 1202, by way of Sir Simon de Burley in 1834 and William Pitt in 1792 to the present Lord Willingdon. Dover's keeps and towers have seen too much violent history to be worried unduly by Hitler.

The Admiral—Vice-Admiral Sir Bertram Home Ramsay, the old Dover warrior, commanded Monitor 25 and the famous " Broke " in the Dover Patrol of 1915–19. He is a man of extreme courtesy, fresh complexioned, with an iron truckle bed in his room overlooking the Straits of Dover. I have been in the Admiral's business-like office, which in the event of invasion would be one of the cogs in the whole defence organisation. Sir Bertram may show you a hole in the roof made by a shell splinter. Charts and instruments are spread out on the drawing-desk. For the times when the Admiral wants to keep on the job the bed comes in handy. It was here that he planned the evacuation of Dunkirk, in a room since known as " Dynamo " because of the terrific high pressure work that went on for ten hectic days and nights and which earned the Admiral his knighthood. Sometimes Sir Bertram walks up and down his ' walk ', telescope under arm—the same telescope that he first took to sea when he entered the Royal Navy in 1898. He is one of the men I would trust to guard the " Gateway to England ". Now he twiddles his glasses. thinks and waits, and I know he thinks a lot and shrewdly,

At the only interview he has given me for publication the question was raised of the lack of German air offensive in the Dover area at the time of Dunkirk. I remember he said Hitler was a methodical man and had probably not yet taken down the book marked " England ". That this explanation was at least partly true was shown by later events. To what extent his failure to rout the B.E.F. was due to the Royal Air Force and to what extent he was less well equipped for the job than we had supposed will have to be shown by post-war history. This is, so to speak, an interim report, and I am already nervous as to how time will show its accuracy.

Anyway, here is one of the nerve centres around which has been built up a complex business organisation for dealing with the biggest business of all—the defence of the " Gateway to England ".

Here, as nowhere else in England, the men and women of Dover and the Services, whatever their job or rank, are welded into one chain, ready at all times for the unusual, otherwise carrying on ' as usual '. The A.R.P. people have just had a meeting to discuss next season's football plans ; the Wrens find time to put on concerts and entertainments of their own ; shops hold ' Remnant Sales ' behind their barricaded windows ; and, above all, the town is prepared for any new blitz this summer may bring.

CHAPTER EIGHT

DOVER PATROL AND THE MEN ON SHORE

Dover's senior service is the historic Dover Patrol. Standing out high and bold on the cliffs above St. Margaret's Bay is the Dover Patrol Memorial, dedicated to the men who fought and suffered and died while serving with that unit in the last war. The exploits of the Dover Patrol during 1914–18 have been told. Those of their successors in this war must at present remain largely untold.

These men have not had the opportunities of taking part in spectacular engagements, but they are doing a dirty, dangerous and unsung job. Many of its officers are men of the ' Wavy Navy '—that little band of ' Amateur Sailors ', territorials of the sea, who have come from all kinds of jobs to serve in the Royal Navy.

They go out by night and day in the dangerous waters of the Straits of Dover. Perhaps they are in trawlers or drifters, small and humble craft from our fishing ports. Their job may be mine-sweeping or one of the multifarious and usually unspecified operations covered by the general term ' on patrol '. No one can pretend that service on the ' Dover Patrol ' is comfortable. But the men of the trawlers are a tough crowd, and they need to be. At any moment a *Heinkel* or a *Dornier* may come at them out of the clouds to bomb and machine-gun.

By night an " E " boat may loom out of the darkness, and now and again the Admiralty have regretfully to announce the loss of a trawler after striking a mine—and " the next of kin are informed ".

Sudden dangers and sudden escapes are the daily round

of these men, a succession of ' incidents ', any one of which
may mean injury and death.

The officers and men of the Dover Patrol have to be
resourceful and ready to deal with any emergency. They
are sailing in seas which may be described as " No-Man's-
Land ". But ashore these men are bright and cheerful.
Among them are dour old Scottish skippers, with iron-grey
hair, who know the worst the sea can serve them. There
are youngsters who have come to the Patrol from such
different vocations as reading for the law, from insurance
offices and from the stage. I am reminded of the wavy-
haired handsome-looking young man who was performing
open-air Shakespeare in Regent's Park not long before the
war. Sometimes he will burst into a quotation and declaim
" Hamlet " or " King Lear " at length. There is the
cheeky-looking snub-nosed youngster, but do not be
deceived by his youthful appearance. He made several
trips to and from Dunkirk, bringing home hundreds of
men, wears the D.S.C., and, like the others, sails in hourly
expectation of being bombed or machine-gunned. The
other day his crew, with those of another trawler, had the
satisfaction of shooting down a *Heinkel*. The men of the
Dover Patrol usually run into some kind of trouble every
time they go to sea. Perhaps shells begin to splash around
them or they meet some other danger.

These are the men who man the fast motor torpedo boats.
We see them daily skimming through the Straits behind a
huge bow wave on missions both strange and dangerous.

Working side by side with the Dover Patrol are the men
we call " Smithy's Gang ",[1] under the control of a Rendering
Mines Safe Officer. They, too, are sailors, but they find
their dangers on beaches and rarely go to sea. But they
are as much a part of the Patrol as the men in the trawlers,
and their story is one that can be told.

[1] *'Smithy' and three of his gang have just been awarded the George Medal.*

The best-laid mines, whether British or German, have a nasty habit of breaking adrift in heavy weather and washing ashore. A telephone report is made that a mine has been washed up at such and such a point or has been seen floating near so and so and will the R.M.S.O. go and see about it.

I have often seen these sinister black globes bobbing about in the sea a few yards from shore, or thrown high and dry on the beach.

They may no longer be a danger to shipping, but they certainly are to life and property ashore. So the nautical equivalent to the Bomb Disposal Squad gets busy. It is the duty of the mine officer at any hour of the day or night to locate and 'render safe' an escaped mine. A single R.M.S.O. may have anything up to fifty miles of coastline to patrol and the problems he and his men have to face are many. Theirs is an arduous, often dangerous job, yet so routine that the R.M.S.O. may deal with a dozen mines after a spell of rough weather. All the R.M.S.O. has to do is remove the detonator and see that his crew cart the mine away. Just that and nothing more, but it is quite enough—and sometimes there are accidents. Tackling a live mine is not a job to be treated lightly.

Sometimes a German mine has to be dealt with. It may be a well-known type or the R.M.S.O. may detect something unfamiliar about the mechanism. Thousands of pounds are saved by these squads of mine salvage men. When the delicate operation of 'rendering safe' has been carried out, the mine, weighing several hundredweight, still has to be transported. It may have to be rolled and bumped miles along a rocky beach or hauled by wire rope to a cliff top, which the party have already had to climb up and down. Even then the rope may snap during the last few feet and the job begins all over again.

British mines salvaged in this way can later be resown,

and as they cost some £300 every mine helps. It is seldom that a German mine is washed up, which suggests that the enemy has rather less control over our waters than the German *communiqués* suggest. I did see one destroyed on a lonely beach. After the dangerous fang had been removed (before I visited it) we had a grand bonfire on the sands. Apart from little things like detonators, fuses and wiring, this type of mine is filled with explosive substance comparatively harmless outside its steel casing. It is packed in three layers, for all the world like segments of cheese. The ' rendering safe gang ', with rubber gloves as a protection against poison or burning, got the stuff out, some forty chunks of it. Then they started a small fire and burnt it in a great blaze that roared like a white-hot furnace, sending out columns of flame and black smoke. All that was left was a trail of ash and a harmless empty casing.

Sometimes a loose mine bobs its way to a place where it is a danger to shipping. There was a case the other night. The tricky job of removing the detonator had to be done leaning over a small boat, with the mine bobbing about in a choppy sea with no other light than that of the moon.

When a trawler is at sea the crew often have the job of blowing up a loose mine with a Lewis gun or rifle-fire. I have watched them at this, bullets spattering the sea until at last a volley finds its mark. But the true R.M.S.O. prefers the more artistic if more dangerous method of approaching it, unscrewing this and that (hoping the recipe is as before) and deftly removing the detonator.

Most of the men in this job are veteran petty officers and men who were quietly settled in shore jobs until the war brought them out of the Reserve. I know some of them very well, and, like the others, they are a fine lot. One was a former professional footballer with a Scottish club, and they have come back to one of the war's odd but important jobs.

* * * * * * *

Backing up the Dover Patrol are the front-line troops who may one day be the first to meet the enemy.

After living so long in a militarised zone, and coming into contact daily with the officers and men, I have reached the conclusion that they are a crowd who will see us through. I know nothing of modern military administration from the inside and little of modern tactics. That is not my job.

I have had the opportunity of seeing a great deal of the army during the last few months—working, living and playing in the Dover and other important coastal areas under practically active service conditions. I have met men of all types and all ages, from the young militiaman of a few months ago to old soldiers of many campaigns.

One night I met a veteran sergeant of gunners who talked about Younghusband's expedition to Tibet in 1903. He had seen some forty years' service. He was playing cribbage, and there, as he played, I saw the figure of the British soldier as he had been seated in cantonments, messes and tents over half the world for more than a life-time. He talked about Lhasa as though it were a trip but lately made. In the last war he had been decorated for " bringing back the guns " from under the nose of the enemy in France. Now he is doing his job as an instructor.

With him are comparative youngsters, men of the new army, who have left civilian jobs to take on the job of working for one of the most highly organised armies the world has known. This army of to-day is a vastly different force from the one that went so hopefully to France and had to scramble back from Dunkirk.

The men who came back from Dunkirk insisted that man for man they were more than a match for the Nazi, and

8

I find it difficult to doubt the outcome of any future meeting with him.

I think of some of the men I know. There is the young lieutenant from a printing works who by all appearances would lead his men anywhere, yet never expect his exploits to appear in print. The fatherly, cherubic-looking officer, with two or three small daughters at home, himself at home in his new job. The man who in happier days played cricket for Yorkshire and is a triple blue. The actor. One of the most professional-looking soldiers of the lot, with a great frame and a deep voice, smoking wicked-looking cherrywood pipes, who was something to do with a bank before the war. I think of the nineteen-years-old lance-bombardier who climbed hand over hand along a frozen steel hawser suspended over the sea from a pier. It was dark and a motor launch packed with civilian workers had engine trouble and was in difficulties. No one ever thought the bombardier would reach the boat without slipping into the sea. But he did, and said it had been nothing when he came back.

There is the young fair-haired officer not long down from Cambridge. I noticed him, unobserved, the other day. He returned the salute of every man he passed, promptly and smartly. When an Alert sounded and there was gunfire, he put on his steel hat, not, I am sure, for its protection, but as an example. He is the kind of man who would carry his gas mask if a civilian, and there are still a great many civilians who do not regard themselves as " part of the show ".

Then there is a major I know, who was just building up a nice little business as an estate agent before the war. He has brought his business acumen to his new job, and they tell me red tape forms no part of his organisation.

This army of ours was quick to settle down when, taken by surprise last summer by the events in France, it found itself, with the rest of the country, threatened by an invading force.

The first I noticed of this front-line spirit was when I saw a young soldier sitting astride a chair on Dover's promenade, close to the little pill-box camp which became his seaside home. A comrade was busy trimming his hair with a pair of scissors, watched with curiosity by an errand-boy, unused to such sidelights on army domestic life. The errand-boy was asked to go away—or words to that effect—by the soldier barber, and the domestic interlude continued.

I once picked up a soldier barber who wanted a lift on the road. He was carrying tin hat and rifle and little brown bag which he described as his saloon. He had been an assistant before the war in a well-known city hairdressing saloon and was now known as the ' travelling barber '. I have had the benefit of an army haircut myself on several occasions.

I have walked down the main street of Dover, which in normal times would be alive with holiday-makers doing a little shopping, and seen instead soldiers at work, detailed to buy vegetables for their unit. Last summer the front-line ice-cream girl I have described was popular with the troops, and for all I know she may be back again this summer. Her kiosk was surrounded with barbed wire, and her stock of spades and buckets and fishing-nets were not in much demand. But her ice-creams were.

Old soldiers of the last war will remember the Nissen hut, which solved billeting problems in unlikely places. It has come back again. You see these round corrugated iron huts in the middle of farm yards or other unlikely places that have become military positions, and you feel you are really in the front line. In the middle of the yard I have seen men, stripped, round buckets, having their morning wash and shave. But ducks still waddle in the pond, the old farmer goes about his duties, and not far away old Tom's new-born sheep are gambolling. They know nothing of war.

A one-time country cottage, at cross-roads, has been renamed " Hotel Adolf ". A concrete pill-box is labelled Piccadilly Circus—the label is properly enamelled and stamped and goodness knows where it came from.

Somewhere else an inn has become the headquarters of a unit attached to a nearby defence post. The back parlour, where the holiday-maker used to yarn to the locals, is labelled " PLATOON H.Q.", and the rare civilian who happens to go in for a drink is regarded as an intruder.

The other night a veteran sergeant-major took me to a dance in a barn only a few yards from the cliff edge. It seemed a grand dance. The ' bar ' was looked after by troops in shirt sleeves, busy with beer and sausage rolls. Through the windows we could see flashes from the French coast as the R.A.F. bombed the enemy the men are waiting for. My host was an old Indian serving soldier and he talked about the song now being sung everywhere —*The Long and the Short and the Tall*. There has been some argument about its origin which I cannot settle, but he said they were singing the tune, if not the words, in India ten years ago. The words went to the style of " A troopship was leaving Bombay, bound for old Blighty's shores : heavy laden with time-expired Tommies, bound for the land they adore ".

The finest sight in the world, this old timer recalled, was, in his day, Bombay from the stern of a homeward bound troopship. Now his view was the cliffs of Calais.

On another night I met a group of gunners off duty. One had got a violin from somewhere. He was a good-looking, fair, curly-haired youngster. He was picking out the notes of *Love's Old Sweet Song* and the other sentimental songs that all Service men love. He had not played for ten years, he said, since he was at school, but someone

had sent the violin and he thought he'd " have a go ".
There was a pianist and a mandolin. It was good to see
the spirit of these men—waiting.

They seem to be waiting a trifle impatiently, too. There
is a real and not simulated eagerness to " have a go ", and
among the men not the slightest doubt about the result
if the testing-time comes. One youngster singing with the
rest had lost his father, mother and sister in a London
bombing raid, but he had not forgotten. There was a
drawn look on his face : he was not long back from com-
passionate leave, and I for one would not like to be a
Jerry that came within his sights.

Peculiarly solid road blocks have become the subject
of soldier's front-line humour. One I passed was chalked
" Don't bend " and another " Hitler's Toll Gate ". Towns-
people living in this militaristic atmosphere have been
quick to adopt the soldier's humour. One shop has the
legend "Haircut finished if syren goes ". The other day
a district nurse was pottering along a country lane in her
small battered baby car. She met a good-sized tank which
just about blocked the lane. " Hi ! " yelled the cockney
driver, " mind my coachwork ".

Sometimes the cliffs of France show up bright and
clear. " The Fatherland looks well to-night ", people
say, but the soldier's laugh that follows the quip would
hardly bring a smile to Hitler—not if he knew the British
soldier's laugh.

In the summer mushrooms play a part in the domestic
life of the front-line soldier. Many of these little front-line
camps are set up in open country and I have often seen
men returning to their billets with mushrooms. They
quickly learned which were the best fields.

But, on the food question, I can say with all truth that
so far as this area goes I have heard no complaints. The
food is good. I was once a guest in the mess, and the beef,

roast potatoes, parsnips, suet pudding and plums made me think there was something to be said for army life. At the risk of being flooded with controversial letters—for obviously there must be many exceptions—I will say that army food is just about as good as the War Office claim.

Many a lonely cottage or country farmhouse now has its regular quota of guests, young men of the front line who are welcomed for a few hours' homeliness.

Not that the life of the men is all jolly quips and good meals. Far from it. They work very hard, because time may be short, and there is never so much done that a little more cannot be added. Some are living in posts that cannot provide the comforts found at others, and in bad weather things can be pretty miserable.

In some places road-houses have become military head-quarters, and one-time rose gardens conceal air-raid shelters and other things. I have seen one with the legend " Parachutists served at all hours ".

The cold snap during the first week of 1941 meant that troops manning Britain's front-line outposts went through a period of severe weather conditions. Cliff patrols, in balaclava helmets, leather jerkins and gum boots had to face blizzards, biting north-east winds and alternating periods of frost and slush. For days at a time army vehicles travelled with chains to get a grip on the snow-bound road surfaces. I have walked along the coast road when driven snow has swept across like fog. But these young soldiers adapted themselves to severe conditions like old campaigners. I have seen enough to know they would do the same when faced with real critical emergency. Little sickness has been reported and the troops are as fit as in summer.

Dotted along the coast in this area are tea and refresh-ment houses, usually closed at this time of the year. They have found new customers among the 'front-line' troops.

There is the Philpotts' place, on a cliff. They have seen nearly everything there of the war so far, and have lost count of the number of planes they have seen crash round them. " Perce " serves in the Home Guard when not serving tea, and Mrs. Philpott bustles round and says " I shall miss all the excitement after the war. I wonder if they'll make me go away if 'e comes."

It became a bit of a joke with us to watch an army lorry draw up outside the café and men leap out like a crowd dashing to a football match and make for the door. " Fifty teas " we cried, and there would be pandemonium, much leg-pulling and chaffing for a time. " Better than serving holiday-makers ", says Mrs. Philpot.

Perhaps there will be the criticism that I am too much under the sway of army influence, that I have seen too much of the good and have been blind to the bad and indifferent, not sufficiently appreciative of the short-comings. I hardly think so. I can only form an impression on facts and men as I have met them. For all I know there may be wide-open cracks in army organisation, but certainly not among the men that form the army. I have seen them in so many different circumstances, and I vow they are the same as the men from Dunkirk, unbeatable. I have used that phrase many times in moments of enthusiasm, and I believe it. It must be true, if you take a line on the people of Plymouth, the Clyde, Bristol, Coventry and other places. We have all read stories of their incredible heroism. Do we all realise that the men Hitler will have to meet are the sons, fathers, husbands, brothers and sweethearts of those who have crawled from wreckage with a smile on their lips ? The " nation of shopkeepers " gibe, proved false at that invasion period, is doubly false now that we have become a nation of warriors.

What sort of reception will they give those who dare

invade the soil of England ?   The misery-making German bombers have crossed in droning droves, and if Hitler sends his men to follow, the words of Gloucester, in " King Lear ", come back to me as I overlook that very Shakespeare Cliff :

> " There is a cliff, whose high bending head
> Looks fearfully in the confined deep.
> Bring me but to the very brim of it,
> And I'll repair the misery thou dost bear
> With something rich about me : from that place
> I shall no leading need."

Those lines sum up the situation in the Front Line.

CHAPTER NINE

THE ARMY

THE army is worth writing about, and I feel the men serving here on the Dover Front (and they are the same as the men elsewhere) have had 'less than their due. They are, in truth, the forgotten army.

I have met these men at lonely outposts on beaches and in the countryside, miles from anywhere. Some are at positions exposed to enemy air attack, for on the coast bombs may come suddenly and unexpectedly.

Once I was inveigled into refereeing an army football match. It was, my friends suggested, either a foolish or reckless proceeding, lightly undertaken, without full appreciation of the possible outcome. I have seen better games, faster and more skilful, but never one played in such deadly earnest. I may add there were not more than half a dozen derogatory boos at the referee throughout the game. I hardly know who would play the keenest game, a team of soldiers or sailors, or one of the Spitfire pilots. I understand that when these lads get into action at rugby they are liable to bring down their opponents with something of the ruthlessness displayed when bringing down a *Messerschmitt*. "Their trouble," one opponent complained bitterly to me, "is that they've got too much damned fighting spirit."

Sometimes front-line football matches are liable to be interrupted by enemy action. On this particular occasion we had expert military spotters on the ground, and the sergeant-major had given instructions beforehand on how we should dispose ourselves in the event of possible trouble.

But when there was the sound of planes and gun puffs in the air not too far away, I did a little spotting of my own.

Troops at Dover can almost see their enemy—through glasses they can certainly see his defences. Their life has naturally been centred round the countryside over which they have to fight. They have been able to see and enjoy what they are there to fight for, which is just one reason why, in their own words, " Hitler will get hell ".

Look in at old Sam Vidler's birthday party, a little country social occasion that stands out in my mind as an etching of England. He lives, with his son and grandson, at " The Three Horseshoes ", a lonely remote inn on the hills behind Dover, a mile or so from the nearest village. There was a full house for Sam's party. He was eighty, if not eighty-one. The reason for the crowd was that we might hear the handbells, that rarely heard country pastime. That was a scene I would have loved to have taken an American to.

Old Sam, eighty or thereabouts, with cheeks like apples, a bit of pure Sussex from Burwash, was the success of the evening, he and his handbells. A number of young troops from a local unit crowded into the low-beamed oil-lit parlour. There were old farm labourers who thought nothing of diving flat into a ditch to save themselves from flying machine-gun bullets and ' shrapnel '—everyone still calls it ' shrapnel ' rather than the more pedantic ' shell splinter '.

As one gnarled old man said to me, talking of a bomb experience, " As I 'eard 'e whistlin' down I dropped flat, like what they say, and it sent a shower o' muck right over me. Rare experience, t'were."

" Aye, it were," chipped in another old-timer, " but fancy old 'Itler wasting 'is bombs on us."

Old Sam's birthday party went with a swing. There was a lot of singing. A sergeant of gunners never tired on the piano and they went on and on. Some of the farm labourers' wives sat round the table. Then came the call for the handbells, to be played by grandfather, father and grandson. Each man wielded different-sized bells strapped to his wrist. The bells were shaken in the air and brought down, in perfect rhythm and unison. The old man was great. When it was his turn to bring his bells in, a determined look came on his face a second before, and then, as though his whole life depended on the issue, he brought his bells down at the right time. *Way Down Upon the Swanee River*, *Annie Laurie* and several others came in the repertoire.

Finally we all sang *For He's a Jolly Good Fellow* and went out into the night.

" Wouldn't have missed it for anything," whispered a young private, adding, " It makes you think, don't it," and I knew what he meant. Here, if anywhere, was ready-made propaganda, and I wish a microphone could have been in that little parlour.

But the real story behind the ringing of these bells is that old Sam's son and grandchildren are carrying on the old tradition in far-away Canada on a set of bells sent specially from the old country.

The story has been told both in the *Chatham Daily News*, Ontario, and the *Blenheim News-Tribune*, the Erieau local paper. It is there that another party of Vidler handbell ringers are keeping that old English art alive.

Old Sam told me the story as he puffed at a cigarette. The handbell ringers of Erieau consist of Sam Vidler's fifty-four-years-old son, his grand-daughter Lily, aged fifteen, and grandson Walter, aged seven.

The set of handbells on which they play was discovered a few months ago in a Dover shop. They were very old, and after having them renovated the Vidler family, Dover, sent them to the Vidler family, Canada.

As a result, said the *Blenheim News-Tribune*, " A most unusual treat was given to the residents of Erieau on New

Year's Eve when William Vidler and his daughter Lily, aged fifteen, and son Walter, aged seven, rang in the New Year under the street lights at the main crossing, with a set of handbells Mr. Vidler had had sent out from England just before the war started.

" Several carloads of persons gathered, but owing to the intense cold in the open they withdrew into the home of Mr. Vidler. The bells gave delight with such old tunes as *Rock of Ages*, *The Chimes* and *Auld Lang Syne*.

" Walter was the highlight of the evening with his masterly handling of the two biggest bells. Mr. Vidler is one of the few remaining bellringers, having spent much time as a boy ringing bells with his father during the Christmas season. His father was considered one of the outstanding bellringers in the south of England."

I came across this story unexpectedly, although I had long known of old Sam and the handbell-ringing trio formed by himself, son and grandson. From time to time I have taken groups of Service men from Dover to hear the ringing. They have always left, to return to ship or unit, with a picture of something they are fighting for.

I talked to old Sam about his son and young grandson. " Aye," he said, " my son Charles learned to play from his finger-tips when he was young. That was why he was able to teach the young 'uns. Why, we used to play all round the villages, and we always rung special for the Jubilee and Coronation and times like that. And we're going to ring special again too when we've won this war, and us here and them over there in Canada will try and ring something special on the same day."

Well, there it is, a simple little story of an old countryman's link with the Dominions, brought about by something that is unusual to-day, even in our countryside.

From where old Sam sits and thinks about the past you can see the flashes of anti-aircraft gunfire and often the noise of air battles has been heard overhead. One of the first machines shot down in fighting over this country fell two or three fields from where Sam lives and there have been a number in the district since. But it does not disturb his complacency.

" Get this war done," he says, " and we'll have a good old ring out."

It would do the people of Canada a lot of good if they could hear a broadcast from the old folks at home in the front line, playing the old bells, singing the old songs, almost under the shadow of the enemy. Next time I want to impress an overseas correspondent with a human story I shall take him up to the remote, secluded " Three Horse-shoes ", which is where the old man and his family live, and let him see a little bit of England as it was, is, and still will be.

The Vidler family in Canada have even contributed some verse in praise of the ordinary men and women of Dover, and every other town, who are ' carrying on '. The lines are :

" There's a man who's not in khaki, but he's fighting just the
    same,
You'll never hear his praises sung, you'll never know his name,
But for dogged British courage we will lift our hats to him,
To the man who sticks to business, to the man who still can
    grin.
To feed the men in khaki must the farmers' sod be turned,
And behind the man in khaki must the factory lights be burned,
And the wheels of commerce turning keeps supplies from
    running low,
So the man who sticks to business will be striking at the foe.
There's a man who fights for England, tho' he'll never fire a
    shot,
By his calmness and his courage he will help the war a lot.
He refuses to be panicked, goes about his work instead,
You will tell him by his whistle as the man who kept his
    head."

The verse is part of a series written for the local Ontario paper by Mrs. Mollie Vidler—and her link with the front line is that she served in Flanders as a nurse in the last war and returned to Canada to marry a Canadian soldier.

So in town and village you find everywhere these strengthening bonds, ties of blood and custom, that are going to make it extremely difficult for the people of Dover or anywhere else to be defeated.

It was in this area, where military and country life meet, that I saw one of the war's strangest air-raid shelters. It was formed out of a haystack, and you crawled in on your hands and knees to a little cavern at the back. The idea was to give protection in the fields to men working there if things got too hot overhead. I do not think it has been used. I've seen ploughing in progress with the sky full of shell puffs. Two of these front-line heroes in a neighbouring valley received the George Medal for their bravery in carrying on under shellfire. They worked in a shell-blitzed area of a south-east coast, of which it was said farmers did not need to plough their fields. The shells did it for them.

I have tried to give and hope I have given an idea of the atmosphere and spirit that exists here on the Dover Front, between men of the Services and civilians alike.

There was that little Christmas affair. There were no family gatherings this 1940 Christmas in the front line, but troops made up their own little informal gatherings. I was at one such gathering, really no more than a sing-song. A twenty-years-old west-country lad was struggling with a stump of pencil and well-thumbed Christmas card.

As he sat on a bench laboriously addressing the envelope to Miss Eve somebody or other, the other lads were singing. Another young soldier had a small paper parcel tied with thick string, and he was wondering how much it would cost to send it because he had to get " one or two more things yet ".   It was Christmas.

That is how I have seen the army, waiting, working and playing, in the last few months.   I cannot describe anything approaching operational movements, but I am glad to have had the opportunity of meeting on intimate terms some of the men who may yet be engaged in the world's biggest struggle.

That will be a grim affair, with no sentiment, no singing, no joking (yet I suppose after all it will creep in somewhere : it always has when the British soldier has been around).

No doubt when, and if, the first Nazis land they will be greeted by someone saying " Oi . . . let's have a look at your identity card."

All this that I have seen for a year is the background on which I pin my faith in these men.   They are unbeatable, like the men from Dunkirk, the men in the little ships and the people at home.

CHAPTER TEN

SHELLING THE DOVER AREA

Suddenly, when all is quiet, there comes, rumbling over the sea, through the town or echoing round the cliffs, a deep reverberating explosion. People who have heard the noise many time's before pause and say, " That's a shell."

Dover's war history, as recorded throughout the world, has been more bound up with ' shelling ' than anything else. It is probable that the town's worst experiences of the war, so far, have come from the shelling.

But although the first news of shelling in this country from long-range enemy guns across the Channel came from Dover, the first shells to be actually fired on England did not fall in that area at all.

Several days before the first shelling of Dover on 12 August 1940, shells had fallen in the Folkestone area. These were the first shells of the war on this country.

The first shells of the war came as a surprise one morning. Some houses were wrecked and there were casualties, a man and a woman being killed. There was considerable doubt for a day or two whether the damage was caused by shells or bombs. We were not at that time so familiar with the crump of a shell. It seemed clear however from air-raid wardens and other reliable witnesses that there were no aircraft about at the time of the explosions. No air-raid warning was on and there had been no anti-aircraft fire. These suggestions led to the belief that the town had been shelled. Later, fragments of the shells were found, and next day it was generally understood that military experts agreed that German long-range guns had been in action. The

Top : ALDERMAN J. R. CAIRNS—MAYOR OF DOVER
Bottom : A GUN CREW
Copyright : M. of I. Film, "Front Line."

censor would not at first allow the news to be given that Dover had been shelled. Later, fairly definite statements were made in American papers that Dover had been shelled by a long-range gun. This was not the only occasion on which Dover correspondents have had the annoying experience of seeing their news trickle out first from America.

Dover was soon to know a great deal more about shelling, with bombardments or short bursts on many occasions.

It is probable that for some time the enemy were using French long-range guns, transported from the Maginot Line on their specially constructed railway trucks. Fragments and parts of shells with French markings have been found.

The enemy's first large-scale shelling attempt was ten days later, beginning with the first shelling of a convoy passing through the Straits of Dover.

I was watching the convoy of eighteen vessels from my usual point on the cliff when there was suddenly a great splash in the water near one of the ships. The first reaction was to look in the sky for the inevitable bombers—we had temporarily forgotten the possibility of shelling. I glanced to the French coast, plainly visible. Suddenly I saw four vivid flashes and knew they were from the German guns. Some seventy-five seconds later the salvo of shells burst round the ships. I did not know it at the time, but my sea-going colleague, A. J. McWhinnie, was in the convoy, which was shelled and later bombed for two hours as it steamed through the Straits. The first shells fell round it as it passed by Dungeness Point.

After we saw that first splash there was a series of flashes, shells, explosions. It was another breath-taking experience to watch this convoy of ships go steaming slowly on with shells bursting all round them. In all some 145 shells were fired but not one found a target. At times the salvoes

9

seemed dangerously near. Still the ships of the convoy steamed on. We breathed more freely as it seemed they were gradually getting out of range. But more batteries of German guns came into action farther round the coast in the direction of Calais. The first shots were fired from batteries in the Boulogne area. Thousands of people watched this new German attack, which was estimated to have cost the enemy some £100,000 on the usual basis of reckoning the cost of a big shell and the expense of firing it at £700 a round. In later days the enemy put many more £100,000 worth of shells in the sea.

When the ships gradually passed out of range shelling ceased. Then the convoy was attacked by dive-bombers off Deal. Our fighters were ready for them and this attack was also a failure. The Nazis were given no time for accurate dive-bombing. Escorting warships presented a magnificent spectacle as they steamed protectingly up and down the convoy at full speed, throwing up a huge bow wave and with their multiple pom-poms flashing continuously. I watched the battle from a hotel doorway in Deal where some women almost wept with fear and emotion as they saw bomb after bomb crash among the ships. There is something very emotional in being the helpless onlooker of an attack like this. I remember one of the women prayed openly for the safety of the vessels. " Oh God," she said, " don't let them get them."

Our fighters, on patrol in anticipation of such an attack, were now busy with the bombers and their escort of fighters.

Suddenly from onlookers there came the cry, " He's down, he's down ". I saw a German bomber dive away from the others. Smoke was pouring from its tail, and after a long dive it crashed into the sea. The air battle continued over land until the enemy were dispersed and scattered.

My last view of the ships was as they disappeared, a thin

grey smudgy line, into a mist of rain and cloud. Another convoy had got safely through. For us, on land, it had been a morning of anxious excitement. As McWhinnie wrote in his excellent on-board account of the attack—" With the finest convoy sailors in the world, we ran Hitler's multiple gauntlet little more than a dozen miles out from his new door-step—France. Germany's long-range guns shelled us in the Straits. His big bombers rained down bombs all round us. We fired six German mines. We ran through his ' U ' boat and ' E ' boat beat. But the convoy made it. Our warships raced at thirty knots up and down the lanes of British shipping, guiding them, shepherding them and waving their greetings to stolid skippers of the tramp ships, who waved back and gave us the ' thumbs up ' signal as each shell missed them."

That was the spirit of the men—the same as ever.

One might have thought that would have been enough excitement for Dover for one day, but Jerry had not yet finished. His guns opened up again that night, this time with a bombardment of the town.

It was Dover's first real shelling experience and a pretty grim affair it was. A salvo of three shells started the bombardment shortly after nine o'clock. Nine more shells followed. They could be heard tearing through the air, and there were great explosions in different parts of the town. It was getting dusk. Dover reacted nobly to this new war horror. There was no panic and very few signs of fear, although admittedly Dover people do not like shelling. It clears the streets quicker than an air raid and everyone makes the same comment. They do not like it because " you never know where the next one is going ". I have heard that remark scores of times. It seems to be rather an understatement.

Still, there was a strange fascination in watching the flashes from different points on the coast between Boulogne and Calais, in counting the seconds and waiting for the ' whoof '. It is easy, after a time, to distinguish between a shell and a bomb explosion. The former is much more ' thuddy '.

It was not easy to find just where the shells were falling. The first damage I found was the wreckage of a church. It appeared that the shell had passed through a stained-glass window beside the altar and exploded inside the church. Windows were blown out and pews were smashed. Shell fragments tore lumps out of pillars. Another shell fell behind a cinema. A third landed at the back of an Anderson shelter in which a family of four, including two children, had just scrambled for safety. The back of the shelter was blown off but the occupants were unhurt.

It is generally agreed that a shell causes less damage than a bomb of comparable size. Shelling certainly did not have any effect on the morale of the Dover people, although after this it began to be an almost daily experience. The only warning people had as they walked along the streets was the first explosion. I have heard hundreds of shell-bursts, and like it rather less each time. My personal experience of blitz terror is that familiarity does not breed contempt, but rather that the more you directly experience the more cautious you become. In those early days we used to walk round the town, trying to follow up each explosion as it occurred. Now, in the event of shelling, I am content to wait until it has ceased.

One of the ' big nights ' of shelling provided a good experience of Dover's pluck. The staff at the Grand Hotel, from chambermaids to manager, set the pace. George would scurry round the tables, blitz or no blitz, hurrying up the fish here, or stopping to remonstrate with a late diner there. Jo, the fair-haired Irish barmaid, would go on handing out drinks and quips, and if we civilians ever felt like weakening there were always the men of the Navy to stiffen us up. One night of shelling there was considerable discussion about taking sleeping kit down to the basement. The girls could go in the billiard room and the men in the table-tennis room. But the suggestion was never taken up with any gusto. The Navy said they were going to bed anyway, and that was that. I regret to admit I made a concession and moved from the top floor to the second, as a colleague happened to be away for the night. I felt rather annoyed with myself next morning when the chambermaid said, quite brightly, " Well, there were a few bumps in the night, weren't there ? " Actually the bombardment virtually ceased about midnight.

Considering the number of shells that have been fired into the ' Dover area ', as it is usually only possible to report them for obvious reasons of censorship, the amount of damage and number of casualties have been comparatively slight. Later in the autumn a special shelling siren was introduced, a double Alert being sounded—the ordinary warning followed by another a minute later. But obviously this warning cannot be given until after the arrival of the first shell.

I think reports of " Dover area shelled " cause more alarm in other parts of the country than the actual shelling does in Dover itself. It is a difficult matter to report shelling accurately for a number of reasons. Some of the shells fall outside the town or in the sea or harbour. It must be remembered that the ' Dover area ' does not necessarily mean the town. Some shells have gone further inland. Many have been fired at objectives at sea.

There has been considerable speculation on the real motive behind some of the bombardments. Those directed primarily at shipping can be understood, although this form of attack is now fairly well proved an expensive failure. I do not know how many shells have been fired at shipping and objectives in the Dover area, but the cost to the enemy in material, wear and tear must be well over £1,000,000.

Sometimes observation balloons have been put up just over the French coast to help the enemy ' spot '. Other times aircraft have been used until shot down or chased away by fighters and anti-aircraft fire.

There have been theories advanced that some of the shelling has been an effort by the enemy to discover the possibility of laying down an effective barrage in the event of invasion. Other people have thought plain terrorism to be the motive behind the shelling of land objectives. The enemy can hardly hope to hit, except by luck, specific military objectives at a range of more than twenty miles.

Edwin Tetlow, of the *Daily Mail*, first put forward in the early days that the motive was plain terrorism. I differed from this for various reasons, but the argument led to the coining of a phrase now part of our local collection of catch-phrases.

" Oh well," he said, " I don't care. I'm going to do some terrorphoning " and went to the telephone. The phrase has stuck. A pair of field boots I bought for the winter became " terror boots ", people we noticed looking up at something became " terror watchers " and now I am doing a lot of " terror typing ". The phrase has spread round the town, and sometimes I am met by someone who says " Come and have a terror drink ". Very childish, I suppose, but one of those trifles that help to cheer you up in difficult and depressing days.

One of the German bombardments which began overnight continued until dawn, again at a cost I estimated at the time of about £100,000. Four people were killed and five injured, a few houses demolished and several other buildings damaged. One shell burst inside a slaughterhouse. It killed four sheep and a piece of shell splinter struck the back of a man's head.

Shelling has produced its oddities no less than bombing. Take a village where three houses felt the full blast of one shell. How the occupants, Mr. and Mrs. F. Clark, remained alive is a mystery. Their house was a heap of rubble. They were rescued, and Mrs. Clark was carried out on a broken chair and taken to hospital with broken limbs.

The next morning Mr. Clark went to his work as usual in a nearby store, carrying on.

In the kitchen of the house a basin containing eggs was shattered and the eggs were not damaged.

I talked to a man who was at Gallipoli in the last war.

" I was never so frightened then as last night," he told me.

Meanwhile Mrs. Tracey was trying to clear up the débris that littered her room.

" I've had two or three goes at trying to clear it up, but oh dear ! " was her resigned comment.

Since then of course thousands of bombed people all over England have faced the same situation with the same calmness.

I share the popular view that ' shelling is worse than bombing '. When enemy aircraft is about you have some idea when and where to expect bombs. A shell just comes out of the empty sky and explodes, and you never know how much nearer the next is going to be.

But when I toured the shelled areas in those early days and on later occasions I found Dover people stood as solid as the cliffs around the town.

On the occasion of the most recent shelling, I had with me a colleague who was seeing its effects for the first time. He remarked on the ' decent curiosity ' of the people. It was not morbid curiosity, but just sufficiently casual. Complete apathy would of course be worse than curiosity.

A woman in a small inn who had suffered shelling or bombing on three other occasions went on serving drinks to civil defence workers who had come off duty, while other workers swept up the glass that lay all round.

" I've been here all the time. I always stick to the job," she said. The main result of this particular bombardment was to kill an old woman of nearly seventy-eight.

Among those in hospital after one shelling was a clergyman. He had injuries to his legs caused by flying splinters. He had seen people to shelters as he always did in raids, and still does, for that matter. Then he heard that some people had been injured and went out into the street to help. As he did so he was wounded. But he said he would be back in a few days and " The service on Sunday will be held in the schoolroom ".

Another man killed was at home with his family when the shelling started. He ran out to see what was happening and was so badly injured that he died almost at once.

But Dover, after the first shock, refused to be terrorised.

There was Mrs. E. Wright, an A.R.P. ambulance driver. Pieces of shell damaged her walls, kitchen and furniture.

" Dad got a piece of shell in his leg," she said. " He was just going to light a cigarette when the crash came. A friend with us disappeared under the table and the cat bolted. But I lived through the last war in this place and I'm jolly well going to live through this one."

Another shelling incident concerned a woman who was having her hair ' permed ' at the time. A shell fell at the back of the building, the room was wrecked, but she escaped serious injury. At the same time people were still quite calmly filing into a cinema for the afternoon show. A bank was damaged in a curious way. A shell came straight down, penetrated the pavement almost vertically and exploded in the strong room. Several garages have been shell-blitzed, but at one, with the roof blown off and a tangle of twisted girders and smashed cars in the background, I still get my petrol. They just put up a temporary wooden office and carried on. The wrecked cars are still in the débris.

Since the first shelling began, from a battery mounted near Cap Gris Nez, the Germans have gradually added to the number of long-range guns. Now, by observance of the number and location of flashes during shelling, I would say there are some thirty big guns mounted in batteries along the coast between Calais and Boulogne. They are of various calibres, from eight-inch to twelve-inch and larger. Some are now probably several miles inland, as a protection against attacks from the R.A.F. These big guns have been the object of frequent attacks, but in many cases make very difficult targets for our bombers. Some are concealed in quarries and forests, and some can be drawn into the cover of tunnels when attacks are expected.

Shelling put Dover on the news map more than anything else. It is the only town in the country to have suffered regularly from this form of attack. Our own long-range guns have been in counter-action on several occasions, but we have fired nothing like the same number of shells across the Channel. Unless the firing is done with a specific purpose it would be militarily uneconomic.

We have however shelled German shipping lying off the French coast, and on at least one occasion a direct hit started a big fire which blazed up in Calais harbour.

Most shelling days are quickly followed up by R.A.F. attacks on the guns, almost at once or on the same night. The whereabouts of the gun emplacements can be fairly well established by plotting the flashes. Then the R.A.F. go over and deliver a blitz attack, and photographs have shown that in some cases considerable damage has been done to the emplacements. There is reason to believe that on several occasions these big guns have been put out of action as a result of our attacks.

Convoys have been shelled on more occasions than the one I have described in detail. In some cases at night the firing has gone on for hours as German guns follow the ships round from the time they begin to approach the Dover Straits until they are through. But these bombardments, noisy though they are, and unnerving as they must be to the men in the ships, cause little or no damage. I have not heard of a ship being lost in this way and even casualties from splinters have been few. It is probably for this reason that there have been few bombardments of this nature recently.

Generally speaking, it is true to say that, in relation to the mass of metal that has been fired into the Dover area, both damage and casualties have been comparatively light.

CHAPTER ELEVEN

MEN IN THE AIR

Iт was during the days of intermittent activity, in the late autumn and early winter, that we first began to see signs of growing British air power. The signs were slight at first, but unmistakable.

Early in October I was able to report that more and more Spitfires were to be seen in the air every day. It became usual to be awakened by the early morning drone of Spitfires patrolling the coast. Right to the end of October and into November the enemy made some sort of show at daylight raiding. But every week daylight raiding became more and more difficult for the *Luftwaffe*. It seemed that the R.A.F. began to adopt the policy of fighting it out with the enemy over the Channel and coast.

It was the first small beginning of the movement which five months later has developed into our own offensive sweeps over France. Last autumn our fighters were gradually beginning to force the closing phases of the Battle of Britain across the Channel. As late as 14 November our fighters shot down more than twenty German planes, most of them before they had a chance to attack. On this occasion most of the fighting took place over the sea.

During the height of the Battle of Britain, in the summer months, British fighter interception was centred along an inland belt in the area of Maidstone, Ashford and Canterbury. By the autumn we were not waiting for the enemy to get so far. Our fighters even in those days were gradually forcing the battles back towards the coast and over the Channel.

Little by little, but without doubt, we at Dover have seen signs of the R.A.F.'s deadlier striking power, power both to defend and attack. Here on Dover's cliffs, it has been possible to read the signs of the gradual equalising power of our air strength.

In the desperate days of last summer to hear a heavy drone in the sky was to be certain that enemy aircraft were overhead, and we were delighted then to see even small outnumbered formations of our fighters. Now, in May 1941, it is different. The most cheering feature of the winter has been the gradually strengthening proof of our new power.

I remember our first real glimpse of this. It came quite suddenly one very early spring day. I saw, as they flew home from across the Channel, a squadron of Blenheim bombers, with fighter escort. It was a striking spectacle to see them as they roared back over the Straits of Dover little more than 3000 feet high. They had been across on one of the first big daylight raids on German bases, and similar squadrons had been seen that morning at other points along the coast. Along the south-east coast that day everyone was talking about the number of our warplanes that was being seen daily in the air. On that day, too, we saw the first daylight fires across the French coast since the days of Dunkirk, when the enemy was in control. The thud of explosions had been heard and, later, dense smoke was seen rolling up into the sky between Calais and Boulogne. It was the first realisation of the promise that this spring our bombers and fighters would gradually take the offensive farther and farther across the Channel with the idea of pinning the enemy back.

No one can foresee how the air war will develop during the coming months. But it is difficult to believe that the *Luftwaffe* can this year expect success in large-scale daylight manœuvres which failed last year against an inferior defensive force. The new 1941 daylight air war tactics have not yet been worked out, but there are various signs and portents that can hardly be ignored by the most cautious. Several times lately I have watched isolated enemy formations, occasionally numbering up to a score of aircraft, strike half-heartedly inland. But they have never sought to press their attack home and have been dispersed a few minutes after crossing the coast.

Perhaps these raids have been of an experimental probing nature, preparatory to something more determined at a later date. It is true that there has been as yet little sustained fair weather, but mainly thick sea mist and driving rain. On the other hand, we have taken much more advantage than the enemy of what fair weather there has been. It is also true that our own pilots who have been over enemy territory on offensive daylight patrols have often found the same symptoms of lack of determination on the part of the *Luftwaffe*. I have met several pilots who have commented on having encountered anti-aircraft fire, but no fighter opposition. No *Messerschmitt* has come up challengingly from the ground. Comments on this apparently evasive action have been made occasionally in official *communiqués*. No one, the R.A.F. least of all, will read too much into this present *Luftwaffe* policy of lying doggo.

The Nazi airman is a wily bird, whether on the wing or roosting. Again no one, least of all our pilots, doubts the quality of many of the German pilots. It is possible to obtain many varying opinions on this point, but the truth probably is that the Nazis have a larger proportion of inferior pilots than we have. I would say that, given an equal number of aircraft of both sides in the air, the largest proportion of first-class men would be among our own. There is every indication that the Nazi airman is at his best when in favourable circumstances, either of height or position. He likes best of all to be able to surprise a pilot in the sun or come down on him from a much greater height.

People who have had much fighting experience tell me that there is no reason to suppose that the Nazis are fond of a battle against odds. On the other hand, they are clever opportunists, as I had the misfortune to see the other day. Two of our Spitfires on patrol were surprised by a much larger and higher-flying formation of MEs. Outnumbered and unable to climb in time, both our men were shot down. They baled out, but one drifted out of sight towards France and the other did not live when picked up by a rescue boat. That was an unfortunate affair due to circumstances that might not arise again for months. I give it solely in an attempt to find a balanced view of what is going to happen in the daylight air this summer. It seems that very important matters concerning the air war on the home front depend on how far the first real test clinches our superiority in the daylight air during the long summer days and nights. There seems no reason to suppose that we shall not remain, as we are now, masters of it.

We, on the coast, remain cheered by the ever increasing strength of our formations. I have seen them recently up to thirty and forty strong, patrolling unchallenged high over the Channel. On the fine days we have so far had the sky over the Straits of Dover has been lined and criss-crossed with the trails of our patrols.

Since that first day offensive sweeps have been repeated time and time again. Even now they are probably little more than experimental, and too much importance should not be given to their damaging power. Their significance lies in the fact that we have taken the lead in delivering the first daylight attacks of the year on any scale.

Our marked tendency this spring is for the air war to go higher and higher. There was a terrific battle recently six miles high over the Channel. It could not be seen, in the haze and distance, but the *communiqué* showed that six or seven *Messerschmitts* had been shot down.

When I first saw air battles, nearly a year ago, they were at an average height of little more than 15,000 feet. Since then the war in the air has gone almost out of sight. One sunny evening recently I tried to follow an engagement between Spitfires and *Messerschmitts*. I could hear the short bursts of machine-gun and cannon fire and occasionally the machines could be glimpsed like toy models. But often they were out of sight, and only when the machines wheeled in the sunlight was there a brief flash, like a heliograph, to reveal their presence. They must have been well over 35,000 feet. The German pilots seem to prefer operating at these great heights and we must follow their lead.

Our coastal patrols of Spitfires are now in the air from dawn to dusk, and you have to be very quick these days to glimpse an action that may develop any moment and be over in a matter of seconds.

The other morning I scurried out of bed soon after 7 a.m. and on to the cliff, following the sinister rat-tat of machine-gun fire. In the early morning sunshine the tracer bullets showed up like pale yellow streaks. Nine *Messerschmitts* had tried a surprise before-breakfast raid and two were quickly shot down, and a third regarded as a probable.

Many more fights are developing over the coastline, and quite often these battles develop suddenly overhead. Usually the high-pitched zooming note of a machine diving is the first indication that a fight is on.

Twice on successive days a *Messerschmitt* crashed in the sea off that stretch of Kentish cliff where for months I have seen the air battle sway, until now, as the Premier has said, it would seem we have command of the daylight air.

I have seen scores crash hopelessly out of control, to take their death dive in the sea, disappearing at over four hundred miles an hour in a whirl of foaming water, and never reappearing.

There is something awful in the sight of a pilot sent hurtling from the sky out of control and helpless.

In the spring of this year then, we are seeing formations of Spitfires and Hurricanes in something like strength, coastal patrols cruising high up and down the Channel. Looking like silver comets, with their short trails of vacuum vapour, these patrols are one of the reasons for a report, " There has been little enemy air activity over the country to-day ".

It becomes clear in these days that our tactics are to go nearer and nearer the enemy hole, waiting for him to come out. Indeed, we do not always do that. We go in and find him.

It is of course still difficult to deal with the single sneak raider that comes from nowhere across the Channel, drops a few bombs on some south-coast objective and escapes, But even one of these elusive gentlemen was caught one afternoon recently. The *Dornier*, thinking it had dodged our patrols for a short time, because the sky is a big place, approached Folkestone harbour, dropped a few small bombs and turned for home. But it happened that one of our Spitfires was in fact in the air, higher than the *Dornier* and above the clouds. Hearing the sound of gunfire, the Spitfire dived out of the clouds, picked up the *Dornier* half-way across the Channel and shot it down.

I suppose I have seen as many aircraft destroyed in action as anyone, and it is always a sight that makes you silent and thoughtful for a few seconds, especially when the machine is in flames or it is clear that the pilot has no chance of escaping. Death can come with such terrible suddenness in the air.

But fighter pilots seem like a race apart. They will not admit they are doing anything spectacular or unusual, and hate the kind of writing about themselves that a colleague once described as " heroic bird-man stuff ". But it is somewhat difficult for civilians on the ground to take any other view, and if ever I meet any of these men the last thing we do is to talk of air matters. They are terribly afraid that anything they say may be construed as ' pulling a line '. I can quite imagine one of them reading, say, the famous Winston Churchill reference about " so many owing so much to the few " and adding the comment " A lot of rot ". I was quite unpopular once when a headline, which I had not written, referred to a certain group as being the ' cavalry of the air '. They would far rather have nothing written about themselves at all. " You shouldn't do that, you know," a man once said to me, after a decorated pilot had been given a nick-name. I think someone had called him " Killer so-and-so ", in reference to his double-figure record. " You people shouldn't do that : it'll make his life a misery." But it is very hard to avoid doing it.

The first Spitfire pilot I ever met face to face skimmed the cliffs and landed in a field a few hundred yards away. I met him walking across the fields. " Not a drop of petrol left, but I got him all right . . . it was my first." He was a young sergeant-pilot who had chased and shot down a *Messerschmitt* over the French coast. He was one of a patrol cruising high over the North Downs to intercept German fighter-bombers, who by this time had replaced the big bombers in an attempt to penetrate our defences. It was the time when the air war had already taken a new turn since Goering had found it too expensive to send across large forces of bombers. The chase was the result of one of those hide-and-seek battles now often played out at over 25,000 feet. Between the zooming of these high-flying

10

" SEPTEMBER 1940." JOHN ARMSTRONG, OFFICIAL
WAR ARTISTS' EXHIBITION
Copyright : M. of I. (Crown copyright reserved).

machines may come a sudden burst of machine-gun fire. It was such a burst, somewhere high over Kent, that started the sergeant-pilot on his chase across Kent and over the Channel until he finally got in an effective burst on the enemy. Then he had the job of reaching home and only just made our friendly white chalk cliff. His leg was injured, but he came in full of excitement and enthusiasm. He had to ring up his station, some distance away, he had to get back, and yes, perhaps he would have just one drink. And would I, perhaps, not say too much about his trip, although he was obviously as pleased as punch at its success.

The first Nazi I saw alive was Ober.-Lt. Werner Voigt, who was lucky to escape from his machine when it crashed just off our cliff. He was a sleek, self-assured man of about twenty-eight who came from Stettin and had the Iron Cross. I scrambled down the cliff and met him just after he had been pulled ashore. He was dressed in blankets, with a British great-coat, and was smoking a cigarette. He spoke with a mixture of French and German, described how first his ' cabine ' had been riddled with bullets from one of our 9600-bullets-a-minute Spitfires and how, winged, he had been finally forced down in the sea by anti-aircraft fire. He was a pleasant enough man to look at, had a quantity of French francs and added the information that he found the French girls attractive. But he was a little bit too confident, too arrogant, and we put him down as a ' smarty ', the type who would delight in machine-gunning a shopping street just for fun. It was easy to see that behind his apparent nonchalance he was a hundred per cent Nazi. German pilots were a little bit more arrogant in those days than they became later when it began to be seen that their master's plans had gone more than a little wrong.

It is one of my theories that a quite considerable unknown quantity of enemy machines, especially night bombers, come to a watery end before they can reach the French coast. Very often we hear strange stories of how someone has seen or heard an unexplained explosion in the sky over the sea. It is never possible to confirm information of this sort. Plenty of these night raiders, perhaps more than we suspect, must fail to get home after being crippled by anti-aircraft fire or machine-gun fire. It is impossible that all the machines seen sailing apparently undamaged through a barrage can have escaped without a few fatal splinters somewhere. It may take some time for damage to petrol tank, oil feed or wings to make itself felt, and many a machine which has apparently escaped has later found itself forced down. That this is no inconsiderable number is shown by the fact that the *Luftwaffe* found it necessary to establish a chain of rescue buoys along the French coast.

I saw one of these in Dover harbour after it had been brought from across the Channel. It was said at the time that it drifted across, but I believe that we assisted in the drifting process. The buoy and its fittings was a model of German thoroughness. Every comfort for the shot-down Nazi is provided in these buoys, which are rather like a large floating tin trunk entered by a steel hatchway in the side of a short round metal tower. These buoys are painted bright yellow because the ingenious Nazi has discovered it is the colour most easily picked up from the air.

Having hauled himself aboard and entered the cabin the sea-soaked airman finds a medical chest, change of clothing, a rubber boat, cooking apparatus and some food. There is sugar of poor quality, coffee and small biscuits like dog biscuits. There are bottles of mineral water, cigarettes and cigars, chocolate and a bottle of white wine. If the water-soaked seasick Nazi airman feels that way inclined there are cards, ludo, halma and draughts with which to pass the time until picked up. There are also writing-pads and pencils for keeping a log.

But it is said that these buoys roll horribly in the slightest sea—there was certainly considerable movement when I boarded the one in Dover harbour.

* * * * * * *

Some of the most misunderstood people in the country, especially by the inexpert observer, are the anti-aircraft gunners, who, apart from the planes they shoot down, are responsible for the damage to enemy aircraft which later causes them to crash into the sea.

The gunners in the Dover area have had plenty of targets —in fact when, towards the end of the year, Lt.-Col. N. V. Sadler, D.C.M., R.A., was awarded the O.B.E. (military division), it was stated that troops under his command had shot down ninety aeroplanes. In face of such a fact it seems ungracious and presumptuous to attempt any mild criticism of the efforts of anti-aircraft people in general. I and my colleagues have seen thousands of rounds fired during the last six months, and we are still asking ourselves the question why so many are ' behind and below '. The real function of the anti-aircraft gunner is more subtle than appears to be the case. Without knowing their object one cannot always fairly judge their methods. Sometimes it is important to divert enemy planes from a certain target area or deflect them to an area where British fighters may be waiting. Error there must be when trying to hit a target moving at 300 miles an hour four or more miles high.

Nevertheless, I would very much like to see an error in front of the target, so that the machine was flying into, instead of away from, a stream of bursting shells. Were it not for the fact that so many gunners have privately agreed with me on this point, I would not presume to make it.

A final word for the unsung Royal Observer Corps, who, on the south-east coast, never have an idle moment. They do their turns of duty all through the day and night, and their watches are usually a succession of incidents. They have no uniform to distinguish them, except a beret and a badge and specially designed tie, yet their work is tremendously important. They are often able to give first warning of the approach of enemy aircraft, plot their direction, and generally act as an intermediary link with both the civil A.R.P. services and Fighter Command.

CHAPTER TWELVE

REPORTING THE WAR

SOME of us are about to complete our first year on the Dover Front. We saw the beginnings of the war as it developed over this country, and it is not impossible that we shall later be able to report some of the closing scenes.

Looking back over those summer days of 1940, when every minute was a fragment of blazing history, one realises more than at the time the real significance of the period. In those days we were too near the canvas to see the picture as a whole. We lived for the adventures and problems of each day. Yet a story was being written in the sky that will live as long as print. We saw but did not appreciate till later the magnitude of what was happening. There was no time to think.

Time and time again a newspaper story had to be abandoned when half written because of some new phase in the day's battle. Everything moved at a tremendous pace. Frequently by tea-time our minds were a ferment of ever-changing facts, and it was rarely possible to give a complete account of the day's activities. At no time was there any kind of official help or contact for newspaper men, which did not surprise the London correspondents, but puzzled some of the Americans. It did not seem to occur to the Dover authorities that any of the sources of information available in London were no use to the men on the spot, which was particularly hard on the overseas correspondents.

We waited in agonies by the telephone, waiting for a long-booked call, and uncertain whether to abandon it and seek some new action, or hold on and miss the new development. We lived by and for telephones in those days. There was only one box in the hotel and there were nightly squabbles and arguments around it. Service people, anxious to make domestic calls, thought we were using it too much, and each of us thought the other man far too long-winded.

Even as late as August telephoning during air raids was a nightmare. I have seen American correspondents, knowing they had the biggest story of the war, frantic at the exasperating telephone delays.

Finally, there came a day when it was impossible to communicate with London for five or six hours and all pleadings with the telephone people were in vain. The Post Office instructions then were that telephone calls were not to be accepted during air raids. That was bad enough, but even worse were the delays when calls were being accepted again.

A desperate telegram to the Ministry of Information, which we all signed, brought instant attention. Three extra telephones were installed for us in a special room at the hotel, and by this time too the authorities had agreed to accept telephone calls in air raids. So the American correspondents and ourselves were happier for a time.

Still, the old original Grand Hotel box did valiant national service until it was blitzed, and then only gave up after a struggle. I remember that Geoffrey Edwards of the *News Chronicle*, covered with dirt and dust, found his way to it in the darkness after the bombs. To his surprise it worked, and he was beginning to tell the office what was happening when falling débris severed the cable and put an end to Dover 230 for good and all.

Some of our bureaucrats, I must say, hardly seemed to realise that it was important for first-rate American correspondents to be allowed to report the Battle of Britain at a time when " Lease and Lend " was far away.

I have always thought one should go out of one's way to help foreign newspaper men, whether American, Canadian, Australian or neutral. We did once have a Swedish woman journalist who was interested in the work of her country's Bofors gun. We were able to show her that this quick-firing gun was doing remarkably good work within its effective ceiling of some 3000 feet. It was very good against balloon-potters, dive-bombers and all kinds of low-flying aircraft.

*   *   *   *   *   *   *

Even in those crowded days Dover Front could present an incongruous spectacle. I have seen elderly men and women strolling up and down the front, quite oblivious to the fact that Jerry might come out of the sky at any moment and all hell would be let loose. In fact the guns went into action several times with a group of admiring civilians round about, until moved off by police and wardens.

We got to know the gunners pretty well in those days, and it was a pint all round the nights they came into " Sailor Pub " and said they had been officially credited with one or more planes during the day. They did not get off duty very much at that time, but when they did it was clear that they were not worrying about invasion or anything else. The whole grim business seemed to be a tremendous game with them, and if they had " had a good day " they were as happy as a cup-tie crowd. It was grand to bask in the reflection of their spirit, and they were clearly the kind of men who would carry on to the last shot or, if necessary, to the destruction of their gun. One of their officers, whom I will call " Captain Bofors ", was a great friend of ours. He was a jovial red-faced man, keener than mustard, who had a clever habit of twirling his cane in a spinning circle round his fingers that so impressed an American colleague that he wrote about it in the course of an article describing the spirit of the men who were facing, and did not know it, a possible invasion. We lived in a strange unreal world then, and I often wish I could have seen some of the thousands of words describing it that were ' filed ' to America.

They were fantastic days and nights at Dover, when our ' field headquarters ' in those days was the porch of ' Dr. Dick's house ', with a welcome covering of coping over it. On the first sign of action correspondents would streak out of the hotel door and make for the corner of the street twenty yards away, overlooking the harbour. If things got too hot out in the open we sought cover under the porch. Some of the cameramen seemed quite hardened to ' shrapnel ', as indeed they are to most things. " Bill " Turner of the *Daily Mail* built a most elaborate camouflage of twigs and bushes on the edge of the cliff to cover his long focus camera and crawled into his little covering with the remark that he was going to be a Red Indian.

A great deal of the area from which we watched the war in those days, when not on the cliff, has since been damaged by bomb or shell. One of the damaged buildings is a Dover oddity known as The Round House. This is a fairly large house built entirely without corners, at the whim of a long since forgotten person who believed that corners were the harbouring-place of the devil.

In this sea-front area too is carrying on the last private hotel in Dover, kept by two sisters who refuse to be intimidated by the dangers around them. They and their few guests are about the only remaining inhabitants of this particular area. They have the Dover spirit to the last letter.

Dover was a strange world indeed in those Battle of Britain days. No one knew what to expect next. The men who were fighting it out for us in the sky were in action all day and every day, and we could see enough of their successes to realise that the *Luftwaffe* were having no easy time.

We could of course only see sections of the battle as it swayed all along the south-east coast and inland as far as London. But Dover was the centre of it all, and it was largely over its coastline that waves and waves of *Dorniers* droned their menacing way. It was extremely difficult to count them. Often they could be heard and not seen until a burst of machine-gun fire would indicate the presence of one formation.

Domestic life in a small country inn may seem an inadequate theme for a war book, but not in the case of the one on the cliffs near Dover that became the temporary headquarters of four or five correspondents when the Grand Hotel was bombed. Some of us went to live there then, but it had in fact been our ' active service ' headquarters for months before that. In fact we had been paying rent for some weeks for the use of a bungalow in the garden. Dover lies in a hollow, surrounded by hills and cliffs, and if any action is going on immediately outside the town, as it usually was, it is essential to get up on a cliff height.

Thus we began to spend more and more time up there. The inn is only some twenty yards from the cliff edge, and commands views to Calais and Boulogne and round as far as Dungeness, as well as some way inland. Very little can go on that cannot be seen from its porch. Sometimes, in the summer months, we had our typewriters on tables in the garden and described events as they were actually in progress.

At a time when invasion seemed more than a possibility Geoffrey Edwards, Edwin Tetlow and myself hit upon the idea of securing a lien on the place as a sort of prepared position. No one knew then, any more than now, what invasion would be like, and there was an idea at the back of our minds that if we had to leave Dover this cliff-edge position would be as strategic a position as any from which to follow events, enemy action and the authorities permitting. It was supposed to be very secret, this hide-out of ours, but later it became a visiting point for many journalists and photographers, permanent and visiting. W. R. Turner, ace *Daily Mail* photographer, was an early member of our syndicate—we said we would let him and his colleague Herbert Mason " sweep out the office ", as we called the bungalow.

It was from this cliff site " somewhere near Dover " that Turner took some wonderful pictures of the first convoy shelling.

There was no idea in our minds then that the inn would become our winter quarters, and that we ourselves would become almost part of the local life, and that one of us, H. D. Harrison, who succeeded Edwards for the *News Chronicle*, would become a stalwart member of the local Home Guard.

" Harry " spent years in the Balkans and Europe before finally having to leave Berlin to oblige the authorities. He was, and is, one of the leading Balkan experts in the country, and one of our little jokes was to tease him unmercifully about the " cafés of Belgrade " and what he knew about the girls of Sofia or wherever it was.

Now, just as he has got his corporal's stripes in the Home Guard, he has had to return to London to look after the Balkan situation for his office, and undertake Serbian broadcasts for the B.B.C. Still, the onions he so carefully planted show signs of life.

I look back at the scene on a recent night. It was a beast of a night, raining and hailing, dark and with a blustering wind. Jack Talbot, veteran of the last war and Home Guard Sergeant in this, and the others were ready to go off on their patrol duty. The wind whistled across the Straits of Dover and the rain beat in from the sea.

Our local Home Guard unit, the only one I know intimately but typical of all the rest, had all done a hard day's work, some in the fields, some in the dockyard, some in workshops or with lorries.

It is possible they will be, with their coastal colleagues, the first Home Guard in the country to challenge an invader, if and when he comes. The idea does not intimidate them, rather the reverse. They, with their friends in the military, and there is a close friendship between the two, are more than anxious to ' have a go '. In fact I may say I have rarely met a more bloodthirsty lot of men. Friendly enough on the dartboard, mind you, jovial company over a pint, or round the piano, but bring up the matter of Jerries and they begin to mutter the most vicious threats and are, I know, more than ready to implement them.

" Cheerio, Tom " came their good-night shout as they prepared to move off on their vigil. It seemed to me at the time that the men of the little inn were chips of the hearts of oak of song. Here, on the cliff edge, fairsquare and bold, was an outpost of the country and one of those nearest the enemy. Some say the nearest. It is in fact a queer experience to stroll outside the door and see the white mass of Cap Gris Nez standing out—sometimes it almost seems a rifle shot away—and see the houses on the adjoining beaches.

" Cheerio, Tom, good-night," came the chorus again. These men seemed good, sound, solid and friendly, as I think most are in this country of ours. But let them see a parachutist or even an enemy tank and I cannot answer for their behaviour.

There is " Mac ", the do-or-die Scot with the Captain Kettle beard, who has joined the Home Guard for the express purpose of ' having a go at 'em '. I should hate to be an enemy approaching his post. These men come in for their darts and their beer and their talk and never a care for Jerry, but I know what is in their minds as they think of the possibilities they may yet have to face.

I remember seeing little Syd Cocks (" Good-night, Tom, cheerio, chum—'ere, where's me 'at—well, so-long Syd, cheerio, Tom ") sitting near the swinging oil lamp in the little parlour looking out across the cliffs. With him was Frank. He plays the drums when we can find someone to play the piano. A friendly, cheerful soul, mild of manner. But he spoke about the Nazis with a bitterness that surprised me (" Good-night, Jack "), and said he'd like to have a " good old go at 'em ", that he would.

It is difficult to know how to divide the time between Dover and the cliff. If you go to one place it usually turns out that you ought to have stayed in the other. It has been a strange assignment, this year of watching the war and never knowing from one minute to the other what may develop next. It has also been a wonderful experience to live at close quarters with the men who are fighting the Battle of Britain. We have seen them all, men of every Service, and often we have heard from them stories that cannot be told yet.

We even have in our inn one of half a dozen kittens—cats now—rescued from a bombed ship. To give his name might reveal an official secret.

When the ship was bombed and about to sink the mother cat jumped overboard in fright and was drowned. But a seaman collected the six kittens and brought them ashore in a suitcase. So far as I know they are still going strong—ours certainly is.

I am conscious that there is nothing peculiar to the Dover people in this spirit, that will bring a flash of humanity here and there to the grimmest side of war. The people are the same everywhere, but it has been my business and often pride to see them on one particular front.

That is why I and all who were with me look back on those mad Dover days of last summer as a cavalcade of great events and small incidents that together makes a picture of Britain at war that will never be forgotten.